Focused for Soccer

Bill Beswick

Human Kinetics

Library of Congress Cataloging-in-Publication Data

Beswick, Bill.
Focused for soccer / Bill Beswick
p. cm.
Includes bibliographical references (p.) and index.
ISBN 0-7360-3002-6
1. Soccer--Psychological aspects. I. Title.

GV943.9.P7 B47 2001
796.334--dc21

ISBN-10: 0-7360-3002-6
ISBN-13: 978-0-7360-3002-1

Developmental Editor: Kent Reel; **Assistant Editor:** Kim Thoren; **Copyeditor:** Bob Replinger; **Proofreader:** Pamela S. Johnson; **Indexer:** Daniel A. Connolly; **Permission Manager:** Cheri Banks; **Graphic Designer:** Nancy Rasmus; **Graphic Artist:** Kim Maxey; **Photo Manager:** Clark Brooks; **Cover Designer:** Jack W. Davis; **Cover Photo:** © Action Images; **Art Manager:** Craig Newsom; **Illustrator:** Dawn Sills; **Printer:** Versa Press

Human Kinetics books are available at special discounts for bulk purchase. Special editions or book excerpts can also be created to specification. For details, contact the Special Sales Manager at Human Kinetics.

Printed in the United States of America 10 9 8 7 6 5

Human Kinetics
Web site: www.HumanKinetics.com

United States: Human Kinetics
P.O. Box 5076
Champaign, IL 61825-5076
1-800-747-4457
e-mail: humank@hkusa.com

Canada: Human Kinetics
475 Devonshire Road Unit 100
Windsor, ON N8Y 2L5
800-465-7301 (in Canada only)
e-mail: orders@hkcanada.com

Europe: Human Kinetics
107 Bradford Road, Stanningly
Leeds LS28 6AT, United Kingdom
+44 (0) 113 255 5665
e-mail: hk@hkeurope.com

Australia: Human Kinetics
57A Price Avenue
Lower Mitcham, South Australia 5062
08 8277 1555
e-mail: liaw@hkaustralia.com

New Zealand: Human Kinetics
Division of Sports Distributors NZ Ltd.
P.O. Box 300 226 Albany
North Shore City, Auckland
0064 9 448 1207
e-mail: info@humankinetics.co.nz

I am afraid that it was rather late in life that I realized that the family was the most important team, and am glad of the chance to dedicate this book to my wife, Val, and my two sons, Robert and Philip.

contents

foreword

The more experienced I became in coaching soccer, at both professional and international levels, the more I came to believe that choices and attitudes governed physical performance. In 1993 my team, Leeds United, won the English First Division championship and, although they were physically gifted, I am convinced that the presence of a core of mentally tough players working within a management strategy was the deciding factor.

Later in 1996, I was pleased to hear that Jim Smith of Derby County had taken the forward-looking step of inviting a sports psychologist, Bill Beswick, to join his coaching staff. As head coach of the England youth and under-21 team, I was also able to invite Bill to contribute.

After three years of working alongside Bill, I am even more convinced of the role that sports psychology can play in improving performance of both coaches and players. As technical director with responsibility for player development and coach education, I am delighted to welcome a book directed specifically to sports psychology and soccer. All players and coaches can gain valuable insights from it.

Howard Wilkinson
Technical Director, the Football Association

preface

I made my decision to become a sport psychologist in the final seconds of a Commonwealth championship basketball semifinal. The team I was coaching, England, was playing host country New Zealand for a place in the final and a possible gold medal.

With 12 seconds left on the game clock, England was one point down. We regained possession of the ball, and I called a time-out. The five players who walked off the court toward me all knew that one of them would take the final shot, the "money" shot, to win silver and give us a chance for gold. Pressure indeed!

Three of the five could not make eye contact with me. The captain, Paul Stimpson, was ready as always to take responsibility if needed, but the surprise was Peter Jeremich, who demanded to take the shot. I was aware that Peter had made only 2 of his 11 shots in the game, but I also saw a confidence in his body language that said, "Cometh the moment, cometh the man."

I gave Peter the shot, the team gave him some time and space, and with two seconds remaining he hit a 16-foot jump shot. We went on to win gold, and I had received a major lesson in the role of mental and emotional variables in successful performance. From that point on, the Xs and Os of coaching interested me far less than the psychology of the players.

I soon began a consultancy practice and was able to combine a personal involvement in playing sport, an academic background featuring psychology, and a love of coaching.

Although my interests extend over many sports, my roles with the Derby County Football Club and the England youth teams have given me the opportunity to develop expertise in the psychology of soccer at the highest level of competition.

Because a sports psychology consultant is somewhat of a rarity still in England, I have spent a great deal of time spreading the message by making presentations and writing articles. I have always found tremendous interest from players and coaches, and many have requested reading material.

So this book represents a natural progression of my personal and business development by providing another way that I can encourage interest in and understanding of the mental and emotional factors of performance. I have tried to capture the important principles I have learned academically and seen many times in practice. To help the reader, I offer many examples of sports psychology in action.

This book challenges players and coaches who have already achieved a good standard of performance to go a step further and embrace the mental and emotional dimension of soccer. All coaches apply some psychology, but this book should inspire them to appreciate the benefits of applying more or employing a specialist.

For players who wish to control their performance and therefore their destiny, an understanding of their own psychology, what Coach Lombardi calls "character in action," is essential. This book helps players achieve a feeling of control—the feeling that one's mind, body, and emotions will do the right thing at the right time.

Although the material is specific to soccer, the principles of human behavior are common to all sports, so readers from other sports can benefit from reading it.

Whatever your background, standard, or sport, this book should interest and challenge you. I hope that you can improve your performance by adopting the ideas and strategies described here—the foundation of psychology in action.

acknowledgments

My first and most grateful acknowledgment goes to the players and coaches I have had the opportunity to work with. We have learned many lessons together. In particular, I owe a debt of gratitude to everyone involved at the Derby County Football Club and with the England youth teams of the Football Association. Much of the experience I have written about in this book is theirs.

My involvement in soccer reflects the foresight of four great coaches—Mick Wadsworth, who first saw the relevance of sports psychology and opened the door of soccer for me; Steve McLaren, who seized the opportunity to incorporate psychology within his coaching philosophy and become one of England's most thoughtful and creative coaches; Jim Smith, who broke all the taboos to employ the first sports psychologist in English soccer; and finally Howard Wilkinson, who watched all this and then gave me the opportunity to work at the national team level.

I must also acknowledge the importance of my membership and involvement with the Association for the Advancement of Applied Sport Psychology (AAASP). I have achieved a far greater understanding of the application of psychology to sport by attending their wonderful conferences. In particular, I would like to single out Jim Reardon, the consultant psychologist for the USA track and field team, for the stimulating and unselfish help he has given me.

Finally, thanks are due to Colin Murphy, Dick Bate, and Steve Round for reviewing the book as it developed, and, of course, for the guidance and patience of Kent Reel, my editor at Human Kinetics.

introduction

The Complete Soccer Player

The mind is the athlete, the body simply the means it uses to run faster, hit further, or box better.

Bryce Courtenay

When David Platt, a complete player and star of English and Italian soccer, was asked to recall some of his greatest moments, he chose two games—games in which his mind took over from his body and he played with relaxed perfection. In both games, his state of mind was shaped positively by important information.

In the first game, for his club Aston Villa against Milan, he was made aware that the Italian club would sign him if he played well. In the second, an international match for England, the manager, Graham Taylor, announced as the squad assembled that Platt would captain England for the first time.

As a complete player, David was able to handle the mental and emotional surge that accompanied such news and channel his feelings into two outstanding performances. For many players the additional responsibility and pressure could easily have damaged their performance.

Such an example shows us the importance of attaining the correct mental state, of being able to control the mind as well as the body, to achieve excellent soccer performance.

This book recognizes that most soccer coaching programs at present are based predominantly—90 percent or more—on physical and technical development, devoting at best only 10 percent of concern to mental or emotional issues. My experience in soccer at all levels has been that the 90 percent has often been clearly controlled, for better or worse, by the 10 percent. Thus the complete player will be one who will search for physical and mental excellence and learn to combine these two for positive effect—"First with the head, then with the heart . . . ."

Demands of Soccer

Table 1 lists some of the important demands of soccer. Players can mark in the appropriate columns whether they think the demands are mental or physical, or both. There are no right or wrong answers. Table 1 is not an assessment but an exercise. Players may surprise themselves by concluding that much of the challenge of soccer is mental.

TABLE 1 THE DEMANDS OF SOCCER

Read the list of key demands in the left-hand column and then check the appropriate column(s) for whether you think the demand is a mental or physical challenge—or both

DEMAND	PHYSICAL	MENTAL	BOTH
Ability to work hard			
Endurance and explosive energy			
Commitment to keep learning			
Competitiveness			
Overcoming fear of injury			
Willingness to take responsibility			
Ability to concentrate			
Composure in the "heat of battle"			
Sacrifice to be part of the team			
Willingness to withstand criticism			
Coping with success or failure			
High level of tactical awareness			
The "intelligence" to make good decisions			

The message is that the journey to soccer excellence—as both an individual and a team player—must involve training to meet the mental demands of the game as well as the physical and technical demands. Because mind and body must act in unison to meet many of the demands of soccer, this book advocates an approach to learning soccer that combines and reinforces the mind-body link.

If physical practice is meant to re-create game conditions, then a thoughtful coach will mention the mental and emotional factors that might well accompany that situation—what is the point of practicing penalties only as a physical exercise?

Five Steps to Complete Performance

Figure 1 illustrates, in broad terms, the steps that coaches and players must take to build a foundation for outstanding performance.

To figure 1 we can add the following:

- Complete performance is multifaceted—you can't break a player into parts.
- Complete performance is relevant to the age and sex of the player.

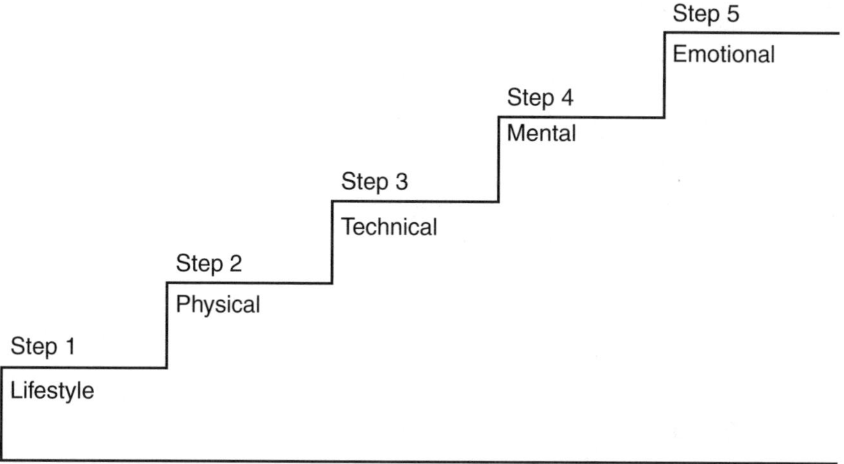

Figure 1 Five steps to complete performance.

- Complete performance is continually evolving. Ajax in Holland, one of the most famous soccer clubs in the world, rates young players with a system based on the acronym TIPS, which they use to evaluate technique, intelligence, personality, and speed. At a recent conference, the head coach for youth revealed that at 8 years of age speed and technique accounted for 80 percent of selection. At 18 years of age, however, it was the intelligence and personality of the player that accounted for 80 percent of selection. The complete player is continually evolving.
- Performance problems can originate from any area. Players and coaches must look beyond physical and technical evaluation to assess underlying mental, emotional, and even lifestyle issues.
- If coaches or players feel unable to undertake this analysis themselves, they should seek the help of experts. Players and coaches increasingly talk to scientists, and they may find themselves the center of a multiskilled support team, as illustrated in the example shown in figure 2.
- Players will never have perfect profiles, so they must work with the coach and support team to recognize their unique style and learn to manage it to the best effect.

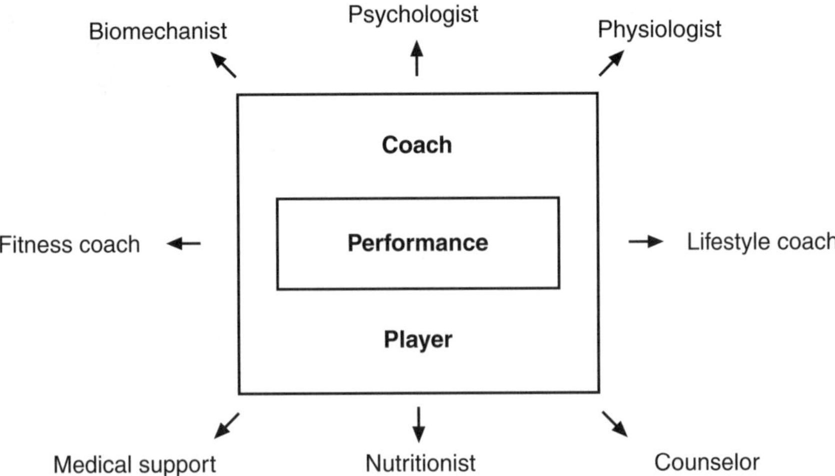

Figure 2 Players and coaches are at the center of a multiskilled support team.

- The art of building a successful team lies in the blending of strengths. Although the Brazilians have a saying that every great team needs a strong man who can carry the piano, the thoughtful English coach David Sexton summed up successful soccer teams as having "the right balance of soldiers and artists."
- The pursuit of complete performance will always be affected by the player's particular situation. When I have exhausted all methods to make a player happy and successful at a club I am working with, I have to conclude that the player should seek a new club. Often the change itself can stimulate progress.

When Jim Smith, the manager of Derby County in the English Premier League, had difficulty with a couple of players who resisted change, I quoted some Hemingway to him: "The dogs bark, but the caravan moves on." He, and they, got the message!

Recognizing the Importance of the Mental Game

The aim of every soccer player, and the coaches guiding them, should be to develop a healthy lifestyle and well-shaped mental and emotional attitudes that allow the player to maximize physical and technical potential.

This concept is introduced immediately to England youth team players when they assemble for the first time, with the message on the board declaring, "Talent has got you here, but it's character that will keep you here."

Throughout the season, the England staff will encourage every player to build a more complete game by recognizing mental, emotional, and lifestyle aspects of performance. A study of baseball players by Ravizza and Hanson (1995) supports this objective:

> The players who get the most out of their ability recognize the mental game's importance and find ways to improve their mental skills. Part of what makes these players successful is their ability to adjust. They are consistently at or near their best even when they don't feel their best. Unfortunately most players leave the mental game to chance, not realizing a strong mental game can be developed.

Journey to Excellence

This book will repeatedly offer the message that the real opponent in the battle to improve mentally and emotionally and live a better lifestyle is yourself. It's really you vs. you.

Once players and coaches accept this, they can use this book as a guide to a more complete performance. *Focused for Soccer* explains what is needed for a strong mental and emotional game plan (physical, technical, and lifestyle issues are the province of other texts) and how it might be developed. Examples such as that of Lee Carsley, a player who achieved success by integrating mental and emotional skills alongside his physical prowess, are included to point the way.

Every player has a unique profile of strengths and weaknesses, so not all the suggestions will suit each player's personal style. Still, enough will apply that each player can develop an action plan for improvement. Also remember that any skill, physical or mental, takes time and much work to develop. As Bill Parcells (1995) reminds us, "The road to execution is paved with repetition."

So read on, learn, enjoy, try things out, and find what works for you. Never forget that the real battle is you vs. you, that only you can make the changes to develop into a complete soccer player.

Lee Carsley Becomes the Complete Soccer Player

When I joined Derby County as sports psychologist, the coaches were quick to point out a talented young player, Lee Carsley, who was vastly underachieving. After gaining his confidence through a series of formal and informal conversations, Lee was able to help me identify the mental and emotional problems that were undermining his performance:

1. Lee lacked inner confidence, which he expressed in negative body language. This projected a "don't care" image that caused coaches and other players to question his motivation and trustworthiness.

2. Lee could not cope with mistakes. He felt so guilty after making a mistake that his overall performance deteriorated almost immediately.

Lee and I then established a mental and emotional game plan that would build his confidence and change the coaches' perception of him. The plan involved many simple but important behavior changes, including the following:

- Taking more care of his appearance and looking like a professional—"look good, feel good, play good"
- Showing more self-discipline by being early for practice, first out on the field, and so on
- Setting higher standards by improving concentration, reducing the number of mistakes, wanting to learn, and improving his work ethic
- Dealing with mistakes and criticism by learning the new recovery skills of emotional control and composure

Lee, a willing student, changed dramatically once he had an action plan to follow. He not only won the trust of the coaches but, more important, developed a more positive and stronger belief in himself. Lee soon became a key member of Derby County's first team and then captain. Later he became a Republic of Ireland international player and eventually moved on to the Blackburn Rovers for a high transfer fee—true recognition that he had matured into a complete soccer player!

chapter

1

Psychological Profile

Player Assessment and Plan of Action

© Bongarts/SportsChrome-USA

It is not the mountain that we conquer, but ourselves.

Sir Edmund Hillary, the first man to climb Mount Everest

One of the tasks I like to ask coaches to do is to visualize and describe the perfect game. The better coaches will quickly and easily outline the physical, technical, and tactical aspects they consider essential. The best coaches, often with considerable and hard-fought experience behind them, will extend their description to include the concept of a winning attitude. They have witnessed perfect games in which the difference in the unfolding contest has been the superior mental and emotional preparation of the winning team.

Interestingly, when I ask players to describe their best performance, I am far more likely to hear about thoughts and feelings. Players often recall how they overcame anxiety and experienced a surge of confidence that fueled an unprecedented performance.

The Perfect Player

Although no player is perfect, it is useful for players and coaches to consider the end point of their work and ask the question, "How would a perfect player react to the many challenging situations that can occur on the soccer field?"

Miller (1997) reports on just such an exercise conducted by women's hockey teams preparing for the Olympic Games. The players worked through hypothetical situations in groups and decided how the perfect player would react.

Table 1.1 translates this exercise for soccer and illustrates that the perfect player possesses mental and emotional skills that match his or her physical and technical skills. There are no correct answers, but responses from players could bring about an excellent team discussion with the coaches.

Performance Problems

As we established in the introduction, performance problems can be physical, technical, tactical, mental, emotional, or perhaps the result of a poor lifestyle. In the past, players and coaches examined only physical, technical, and tactical issues in relation to performance

TABLE 1.1 THE PERFECT SOCCER PLAYER — PLEASE COMPLETE

Situation	The Perfect Player Responds By
Inconsistent refereeing	
Unfair criticism	
Being a substitute coming on	
Recovery from injury	
A run of defeats	
Making mistakes	
Mistakes by teammates	
Crowd pressure	
Receiving a yellow card	
Being substituted from the game	
Going a goal down	
Going a goal up	
The challenge of the "big" game	
"Dips" in form	
Intimidation by opponents	

problems, but we are now becoming more aware of the potential impact of mental, emotional, and lifestyle issues. One note of caution is that the player and coach must be sure that a biological or medical condition is not the cause of the behavior weakness. An important part of my work is to review players' physical condition with the team doctor before I concentrate on potential mental and emotional factors. The Rory Delap case study illustrates the need to be cautious in the diagnostic stage.

Rory Delap Gives Us Food for Thought

The case of Rory Delap, a young player at Derby County, illustrates that performance problems can be multifaceted and that coaches should be wary of making quick judgments.

Rory plays wingback, a position that makes great physical demands on the player, requiring both endurance and explosive energy. After an excellent start to the season, Rory suddenly lost form, especially in the second half of games when the frequency and length of his supporting runs would diminish.

While the coaches privately discussed Rory's loss of confidence, lack of ability, inability to understand tactics, and a host of other potential reasons, I approached Rory and asked him his views. What emerged was a problem of nutrition, easy to understand and easy to cure. Rory had recently left the club's hotel to live in his first purchased house, and he couldn't cook! As his nutritional intake plunged, so did his performance. He was running on empty! A series of arrangements, including a telephone call to his mother, were put in place, and the problem resolved itself.

In observing players it is important that I help the coaches by identifying reasons other than physical or technical that might be adversely affecting a player's performance. To do this, I need to observe players at practice and in games, when I may be the only spectator not watching the ball. Most important is that I build relationships with players so they can feel comfortable in sharing problems with me.

Performance problems can often cause an emotional overreaction. Players and coaches must be careful not to jump to conclusions. Employing a series of questions might help identify the true cause of the problem:

Q1. Is this a "can't do" or a "won't do"? If the former, the problem is clearly technical; if the latter, it's one of attitude.

Q2. When and how do problems occur?

Q3. Are problems restricted to one element of performance, or do they affect several areas of play?

Q4. What thoughts and feelings does the player associate with the problem?

Q5. Are problems the result of pressure? Is the player OK in practice but not in the game?

By such deduction, as shown in the Rory Delap example, players and coaches can be more objective and can more accurately and quickly identify the causes of performance problems.

Of course, to understand performance problems you have to understand performance. I constantly urge young sports psychologists to work on understanding the game and what players and coaches are trying to achieve. I once sent a rather naive student to observe a local semiprofessional club. After the game, the coach asked for his input. The student immediately criticized the coach for not taking No. 10 off at halftime.

"Why?" asked the coach.

"He only touched the ball five times," said the student.

"But he scored twice," said the coach as he ended the conversation!

Player Assessment—Mental and Emotional Strengths and Weaknesses

Before a player plans a route to becoming a more complete player, he or she needs to assess present strengths and weaknesses. Having identified the priorities for change, the player can collaborate with the coach to establish a series of short- and long-term goals.

The basis of my assessment is that player behavior can be a function only of the player or the situation, therefore

$$\text{Behavior} = \text{Personality} \times \text{Environment}$$

If it's a personality issue, the key question is whether it's a "can't do" or a "won't do." The former is a skill problem, the latter an attitude problem. If it's down to the environment, the issue is whether the player can change to fit the situation or whether we can change the situation to fit the player.

The assessment exercises presented here are quick, easy to understand, and acceptable to a soccer culture that can be wary of such tests. The subjective nature of these assessments means that we must take care in interpreting the responses, but I have found a general consistency between the theoretical response and the observed performance. Botterill and Patrick (1996) agree:

> In the end, though, no one knows better than you, so your perceptions of your psychological skills, strengths, and limitations in key situations should usually be the basis of development initiatives and priorities, and will probably prove to be fairly accurate.

At the very least, performing such an assessment can open lines of communication between player and coach.

Assessment by Triangulation

When I joined the staff of the England under-18 soccer team, the head coach, Howard Wilkinson, had the problem of selecting a few from the many available for trial. Each player was supported by one recommendation. I suggested that we increase the number of evaluations to three, that we use the process of triangulation. If three coaches, one of whom had to be a football association regional coach, were consistent in their opinion of a player, we would be more likely to obtain a valid assessment.

Players should be wary of one opinion of their performance but should strongly consider three consistent views.

Assessment by Hardware-Software Rating

Player performance is a combination of physical and mental skills. Players and coaches often want a quick way to determine the relative strengths and weaknesses of these areas. As a way of explaining the need to integrate physical and mental skills, I often compare players to a computer. The physical skills are the hardware, and the mental skills are the software. Performance requires both, and the well-known computer phrase "Rubbish in, rubbish out" highlights the need for developing a player's mental state.

Figure 1.1 graphs the relationship between a player's hardware and software skills. Coaches are asked to assess each on a level of 1 (poor) to 10 (excellent). Clearly, this is a quick and rough guide, but informed assessors can provide useful information on which to base future work.

Complete Player Assessments

The introduction to this book emphasized that because complete performance in soccer is multifaceted, a weakness in one area can

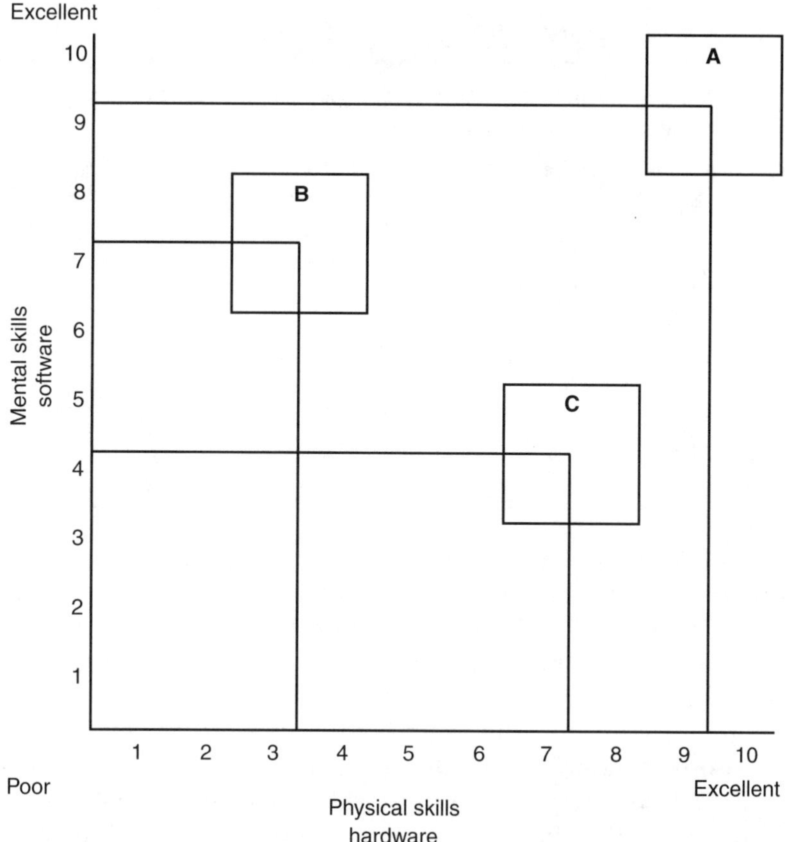

Figure 1.1 The relationship between a player's hardware and software skills. Player A is a complete player with no significant weaknesses; player B is mentally strong with possible physical weaknesses; and player C is physically strong but may have mental weaknesses.

lead to an overall performance problem. Table 1.2 asks the players to assess themselves on the five elements of complete performance. Again, the route to greater validity is to increase the number of informed players and coaches making the assessment.

At a recent conference I asked over 100 coaches to rate player A and player B (the examples in our table 1.2), both at the time English national team players. The average of the responses clearly shows player A to be a complete player but perhaps one who needs to watch a tendency to overreact emotionally. Player B is extremely gifted technically but incomplete holistically. In his case, a poor lifestyle might cause physical, mental, and emotional damage. The superb technical ability of player B subsequently got him to international level, but his character could not keep him

TABLE 1.2 COMPLETE PLAYER RATING SCALE

Assess each aspect of performance on a scale of 1 to 10 using high scores to indicate excellence. Players A and B are examples.

ASPECT OF PERFORMANCE	PLAYER A	PLAYER B	YOUR SELF-ASSESSMENT	COACH'S RATING OF YOU
Physical	9	6		
Technical	8	10		
Mental	9	6		
Emotional	7	5		
Lifestyle	9	4		
Total	42	31		

there. This story reinforces our message to young players that talent opens the door, but character gets them through to the other side.

To develop an action plan for improvement, players should assess themselves and compare their rating with that given by the coaches. This is not a foolproof exercise, of course, and players and coaches may alter the weighting of the elements or interpret the responses more specifically according to personality or position played. Be wary also of lifestyle assessments that may be hearsay rather than fact. What is true, though, is that this exercise raises awareness and can give early warning signals about particular elements of performance.

Winning Attitudes Profile

After reviewing many case studies in soccer I put together 24 key questions that form a picture of the mental and emotional skills of a player who has what we know as a winning attitude.

Again, the questionnaire in table 1.3 relies mainly on self-assessment (the coach can also complete it from his or her perspective), but I have usually found it accurate in highlighting strengths and weaknesses.

Those who might like to understand more about the winning attitudes evaluation should know that the questions are clustered around three key psychological areas—self-concept, motivation, and mental toughness. By separating the scores for these clusters, players and coaches can more specifically identify any weaker response.

TABLE 1.3 WINNING ATTITUDES—A SELF-RATING QUESTIONNAIRE

Here are some statements that coaches and players can use to describe the psychological qualities needed for excellence. Rate yourself for each statement. A score of 5 would mean the statement is definitely true of you, and a score of 1 would mean it is absolutely not true of you. Scores between 1 and 5 would reflect partial truths. The total score is useful only when compared within the group; more important is increasing self-awareness of weaknesses.

STATEMENT	FALSE				TRUE
1. I am always confident in my abilities.	1	2	3	4	5
2. Challenge is fun.	1	2	3	4	5
3. I always see myself performing at my best.	1	2	3	4	5
4. I keep highs and lows in equal perspective.	1	2	3	4	5
5. You can rely on me to stay self-disciplined.	1	2	3	4	5
6. I am willing to sacrifice to achieve.	1	2	3	4	5
7. I enjoy every practice and game.	1	2	3	4	5
8. I am always cool under pressure.	1	2	3	4	5
9. I feel good about myself as a player.	1	2	3	4	5
10. I know my strengths and weaknesses.	1	2	3	4	5
11. I recover from mistakes well.	1	2	3	4	5
12. Distractions never affect my game.	1	2	3	4	5
13. I am willing to work as hard as it takes.	1	2	3	4	5
14. I will take risks when the situation is right.	1	2	3	4	5
15. I practice proper relaxation and recovery methods.	1	2	3	4	5
16. I respond well to useful criticism.	1	2	3	4	5
17. I push harder even when it hurts.	1	2	3	4	5
18. I enjoy being part of a team effort.	1	2	3	4	5
19. I never allow negative thinking in games.	1	2	3	4	5
20. Practicing with intensity is important to me.	1	2	3	4	5
21. I recover well from setbacks in the game.	1	2	3	4	5
22. I will persist until I achieve.	1	2	3	4	5
23. I always take responsibility for my actions.	1	2	3	4	5
24. I need to be the best I can be.	1	2	3	4	5

(continued)

TABLE 1.3, *(continued)*

SCORING BOX	YOUR TOTAL	COACH'S TOTAL	TEAM AVERAGE
All questions			
Self-concept			
Motivation			
Mental toughness			

TABLE 1.4 WINNING ATTITUDES – INDIVIDUAL PROFILE

Player's Name: LEE CARSLEY

PSYCHOLOGICAL FOCUS	PLAYER SCORE (MAX. 40)	COMMENTS
Self-concept "The way you view and value yourself as a player."	23	To your credit you recognize the problem and give yourself the lowest lowest score in the squad. The coaches feel this is holding you back and you must become more positive about yourself.
Motivation "Your willingness to pay the price."	35	A good score which reflects your desire to do well. The coaches also praise your commitment and pride in performance.
Mental Toughness "The strength of your focus, the durability of your concentration."	31	There is concern about your ability to handle pressure with emotional control. In the position you are being asked to play, it is important to combine passion with discipline and composure.

PLAYER ACTION PLAN: THE KEY IS BELIEF IN YOURSELF

1. You have to be more positive about yourself and surround yourself with positive influences.
2. Set yourself small, achievable targets for this season to improve your confidence but, just as importantly, the confidence of others in you (e.g. look good, feel good, play good).
3. Practices, and your attitude to them, are very important in changing attitudes towards you.
4. When you make errors or lose control emotionally, try to remember what caused them and create a plan not to let them happen again.
5. Don't get depressed—you have achieved a great deal so far and much of what is wrong here can only be changed by experience.
6. When you get forward on runs you have to express commitment and the conviction you can (a) get into the box, and (b) score. Set yourself targets.
7. Be patient and take the long-term view of your career.

The clusters are the following:

- Self-concept—questions 3, 4, 9, 10, 15, 16, 18, 19
- Motivation—questions 1, 6, 7, 13, 17, 20, 22, 24
- Mental toughness—questions 2, 5, 8, 11, 12, 14, 21, 23

Naturally, some of the most interesting talking points are the differences of opinion between the players' rating of themselves and their rating by the coaches.

In the introduction we looked at how Lee Carsley got the message about mental and emotional development. Lee's rapid and exciting progress began after he completed the winning attitudes questionnaire and began to discuss with me how to improve his low self-concept and poor emotional control. A compelling demonstration of the improvement in Lee's self-concept is that he agreed to share his first results, table 1.4, with you.

Creating the Thinking Player

An important by-product of engaging in assessment exercises is that the player begins to think about his or her performance and take ownership of both physical and mental development.

One of the benefits of having a sports psychologist working with a soccer club is that players will become more involved in their performance.

1. Players will be asked to employ self-reference—to judge their own performance, to evaluate their strengths and weaknesses, and to come to terms with their attitudes and feelings rather than simply listening to the coach or parent telling them how they should think.

2. Players will engage in self-reflection. Aided by video analysis and comments of the coaches, the player will reflect on his or her performance and ask questions such as the following:

    - What happened?
    - What was I thinking and feeling at the time?
    - What was good (or bad) about the experience?
    - What else could I have done?
    - If it happened again what would I do?
    - If I wanted to change this behavior, could I?

We know already that the battle to attain excellent mental and emotional skills is you vs. you. These exercises force players to confront themselves and accept responsibility for any progress or change. Using this process builds a high level of intrinsic motivation. Players want to achieve progress for themselves rather than relying on the urgings of a coach or parent, which marks an important stage on the way to mental toughness.

This process is especially important to goalkeepers and strikers who are the most vulnerable to mental and emotional stress. The goalkeeper cannot hide on the soccer pitch—the keeper either saves the shot or doesn't. Even if it's not the keeper's fault, he or she will have to pick up the ball from the back of the net. Similarly, all can clearly see that the striker either scores or misses with the chances he or she is given. For these players, self-referencing and self-reflection are important methods of coping with stress.

Developing an Action Plan

Your plan of action to become a more complete player or coach began when you picked up this book. It now continues as you use these quick, easy measures to assess mental and emotional strengths and weaknesses.

You should understand that psychological skills are not magic. It isn't true that some people have them and some don't. Anyone can learn psychological skills at any time and in most places, but like physical skills, effective learning requires good early instruction, repetition, and perseverance. This book aims to raise your awareness of the essential importance of mental and emotional skills in your performance and then to provide you with that good early instruction.

As you proceed through the book you will find many suggestions for improving your mental strength. I suggest that you adopt the following routine in incorporating these ideas into your training and performance philosophy.

- **Assess**—use the tools offered to determine your weaknesses.
- **Set goals**—decide what you would like to achieve and identify a progressive series of small and relatively easily achieved steps that will take you there.
- **Visualize**—see yourself as you want to be and check what it will feel like. Use nonactive moments with the team such as when traveling on the bus.

- **Practice**—act out your visualization and implement it. Decide that "if that happens, then I will respond by such a behavior." Forgive yourself for your mistakes. As with all learning, you will use a trial-and-error pattern. Learning to recover is itself an important skill. Players should commit to practicing mental skills in all aspects of their lives. For example, they can practice composure and arousal-frustration control just as easily in a traffic jam as at training.
- **Monitor**—constantly check your progress and listen to the comments of those around you. Are they seeing a change? Watch videos of yourself in action and reflect on your performance.
- **Automate**—a relevant saying is that "habits save you in big games." Repeat until you have a new and positive habit.
- **Enjoy**—your new behavior will boost your confidence. Reward yourself by enjoying your status as a more complete player.

To help you understand and become familiar with this process, examine the many case studies in this book and check them against this system for developing mental skills.

Integrating Physical and Mental Skill Development

Although in some situations players can practice mental skills in isolation, there are clear benefits when the mind and body link can be positively reinforced in practice and competition. Jim Reardon (1992) expresses the view of the sports psychology team responsible for the USA track and field team:

> Specifically, we believe that psychological skills training is most effective when it is interwoven into the physical training regimen on a continual basis. The failure to incorporate these skills/abilities into training opens the athlete up to a variety of disruptions in performance. How many times have you seen athletes who were physically prepared, struggle through competitions self-consciously burdened by worry and doubt?

An excellent example was devised by Anson Dorrance, coach of the highly successful women's soccer team at the University of North Carolina. The strategy was simple: get great players and add psychological strength.

To achieve this, the coaches integrated a mental training program with a vigorous physical program. They assessed each drill for how it would develop psychological strength as well as how it would build physical capacity. This produced an intense and exacting physical schedule in which focus, intensity, desire, competitiveness, and mental toughness were essential to survival and success. Here, "the muscles were the slaves of the brain."

Such integration, plus the policy of always playing the toughest opponents possible, made the women players of North Carolina confident, highly competitive, and able to cope with the stresses of the big game. The coaches clearly demonstrated a commitment to enhancing the mental and emotional functioning of the players and built this into every aspect of their training and competition.

To prevent inadequate mental preparation from undermining excellent physical preparation, coaches should integrate mental skills training into physical routines whenever possible. Figure 1.2 illustrates a model practice that aims to achieve this. If the drill was a 3 vs. 1 "keep ball" practice, the coach, besides reinforcing players' technical skills, could use the opportunity to program relevant software messages such as concentration on and off the ball, composure ("control the defender"), challenge ("accept the challenge"), communication, managing mistakes, and maintaining determination to succeed. All are essential aspects of successful, complete performance.

Summary

This chapter proposes that the perfect player will have mental and emotional skills to match his or her physical and technical prowess. In that sense, performance problems of nonperfect players are as likely to be mental or emotional as they are to be physical or technical. Players and coaches must learn to identify strengths and weaknesses in a valid and objective manner.

The chapter proposes some simple, quick, and reasonably reliable forms of assessing players' mental and emotional strengths, suggesting that such assessments can at least generate a meaningful discussion between player and coach. Players who wish to improve all aspects of their performance are encouraged to use self-reference and self-reflection to take control of their performance.

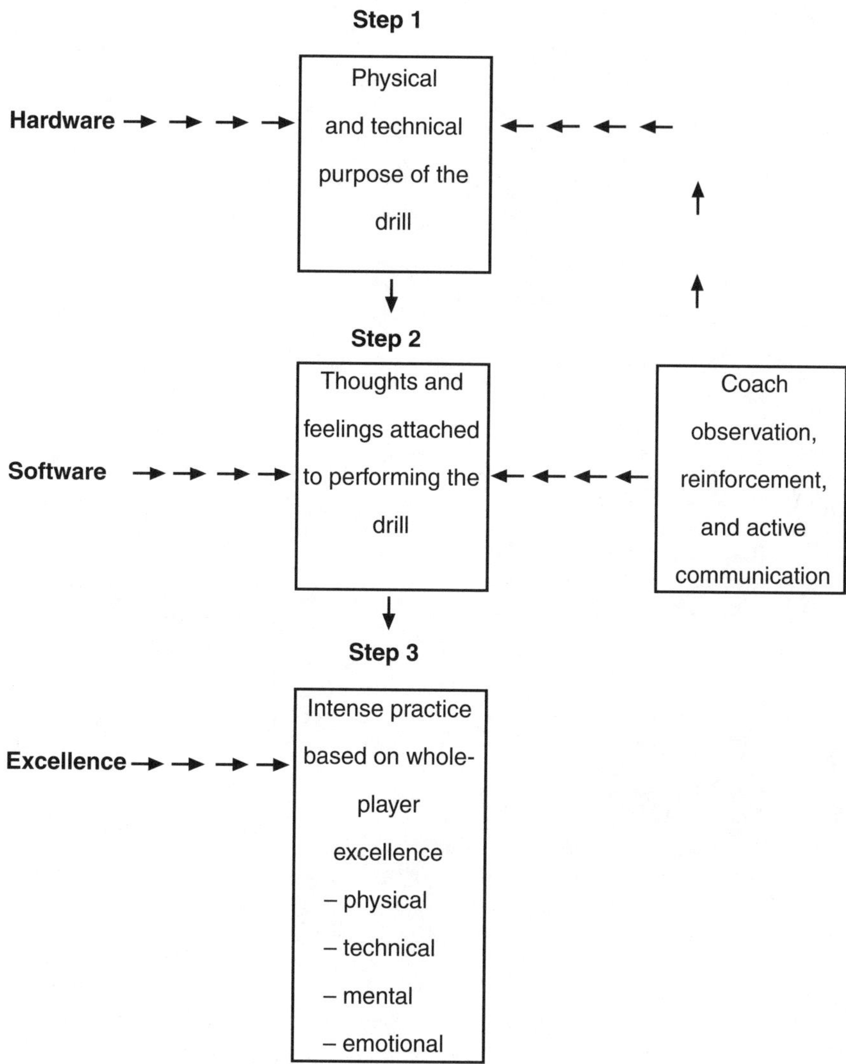

Figure 1.2 A model practice integrating physical and mental aspects of performance.

Finally, players and coaches are offered a plan of action for developing their mental and emotional skills. The ideal method is to integrate mental and emotional skill learning with every aspect of physical and technical learning. Each practice then provides players with the most comprehensive holistic learning experience.

chapter

2

Confidence

Positive Mental Energy to Perform and Persist

They are able because they think they are able.

Virgil

Some players walk on to the pitch and others jog, but Paul Murray used to burst on to the field in a positive and dramatic fashion. When I asked him why, Paul told me that in all his life the soccer pitch was where he felt happiest! At the same club, Carlisle United, a young substitute, Lee Dickson, was asked whether he was ready to go into the game. Lee's epic reply was, "Boss, I was born ready!"

If only I could bottle such confidence—a young man's belief that he could handle the challenge of soccer. The more I work alongside junior, senior, and international players, the more clearly I see that soccer constantly assaults player confidence. I have come to understand that confidence lies at the heart of successful performance.

Figure 2.1 illustrates the variety of confidence-threatening situations that regularly face players and coaches. The central purpose of my work is to help players, coaches, and teams achieve a

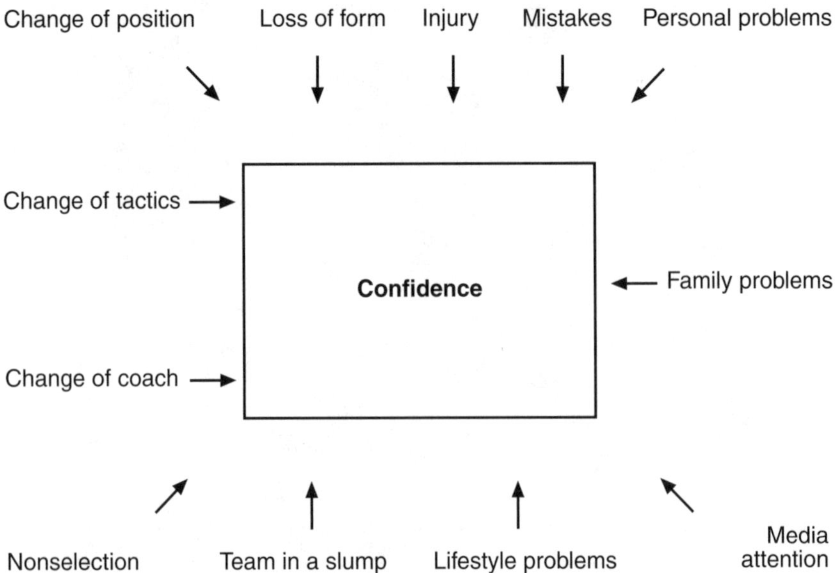

Figure 2.1 Situations that threaten the confidence of both players and coaches.

state of confidence that can stimulate consistently high performance levels and withstand the inevitable setbacks.

Being able to recover from defeat is an essential characteristic of confidence. This capability has been a prime factor in the relative success of Derby County in the past three seasons, during which the team has never lost more than three games in a row.

Confidence Is a Choice

The journey to becoming a more complete player begins by building confidence and then learning to maintain it after setbacks. When players or coaches describe themselves as under pressure, they are really identifying a lack of confidence in dealing with a situation. With confidence, we expect success. Learning something new, like building the mental game plan described in this book, becomes a challenge rather than a problem.

Confidence, though, is a choice—you have to choose to become confident. When I talk to younger players I illustrate this point by describing (and acting out!) the behavior of two parrots, one perched on each shoulder. One of them is the positive parrot, constantly urging the player to face up to the challenge, saying, "You can do it." The other is the negative parrot, incessantly warning the player, "You can't do this." Clearly, you choose which parrot you listen to.

Once you have made the choice, and it may be an everyday decision, you must take responsibility for your actions. Successful players build strong inner confidence by concentrating on their contribution to success or failure. Rather than blaming someone or something else—a sign of insecurity—they take responsibility and see setbacks as part of a learning curve, not a disaster that could damage confidence.

I recall an outstanding basketball player who, with his team losing by one point and no time left on the clock, missed two foul shots. His team lost the national championship. When interviewed he immediately took responsibility: "Sometimes in sport you are a hero, sometimes a bum. Today I am a bum, tomorrow I will be a hero."

With this perspective, the player chose to accept the setback and cause no lasting damage to his confidence—he still felt himself to be a great player.

Similarly, the most important self-talk for a player who misses a chance on goal is the phrase "I'll get the next one," immediately ensuring that the disappointment of the miss does not damage the confidence of the next strike.

Characteristics of Confidence

One of the keys to managing a successful international team is the ability to make quick judgments about a player's ability to cope with the demands of international competition. Judging physical readiness is easier than judging mental readiness, so the staff will look for clear messages, both verbal and nonverbal, that the player is confident in his or her ability to succeed at this level.

Players high in confidence offer such messages by

- having high self-belief—a "can do" attitude;
- projecting a positive image—always showing good body language;
- enjoying competition and smiling;
- not worrying unduly about failure or consequences;
- being self-dependent, not seeking to blame others;
- staying calm and collected, showing good self-control;
- talking to themselves and others in an encouraging, positive way;
- concentrating well, both in training and in matches;
- having no need to impress others; and
- accepting themselves while understanding their strengths and weaknesses.

All these characteristics reflect a player's confidence in his or her ability to cope with the challenge of soccer, which initiates a chain reaction that provides a high level of energy—the fuel of positive performance. Table 2.1 shows the relationship between confidence and positive energy, illustrating that the player's state of mind and confidence is crucial to successful performance.

One of the ways I help coaches is by using my freedom from specific responsibility in practice to observe players and check their body language, comments, and performance for clues to their general level of confidence. I once remarked to Coach Steve McLaren after practice that I felt that Derby's Italian star, Stefano Eranio, was a little down in attitude. The coach called him at home that evening, the player was delighted, and a two-hour conversation put Eranio's world right.

TABLE 2.1 RELATIONSHIP BETWEEN CONFIDENCE AND ENERGY

	PLAYER A	PLAYER B
Attitude	Confident	Lacking confidence
Emotions	Excited, vigorous	Anxious, frustrated
Energy	Positive	Negative
Potential performance	Successful	Unsuccessful

Steps to Building Confidence

Although the building of confidence is an everyday task, players should consider certain key steps to find what works for them.

Stay in the Game

When Jackie Stewart, the famous Scottish racing driver, allowed the television cameras into his home, viewers quickly noticed that he had retained only one trophy from the many he had won. Jackie explained that he had won that trophy in a race that had taught him an invaluable lesson early in his career. He had been lying in seventh position with six laps to go, had given up hope, and was cruising. By the end of the race all six of the cars in front had withdrawn with mistakes or problems. Jackie had learned that by staying in the game and competing for as long and as hard as he could, he might make his own luck.

Confidence is built on experience, with the greatest boost going to the player having the knowledge that he or she has been there before and knows what to expect. Players have to be willing to go through the fire of fears, mistakes, defeats, and criticism to build the foundation of experience they need for confidence at the highest levels.

The next time you watch an Olympic champion celebrate success, remember that many of them failed in their first appearance at the Games. But they had been through the fire, had learned from their mistakes, and had stayed in the game before succeeding at the second or even third attempt. Do you think they feel it was worth it?

Commit to Good Preparation

Confidence comes from success, and success in soccer is more likely if you run out on the pitch knowing you have done everything you could to prepare for situations that might bring pressure. Clearly, lack of preparation can result in the stress (absence of confidence) of not being able to handle such pressure. "If you are not preparing to win, you are preparing to fail," is a phrase often quoted. Good coaches take the view that if they have prepared properly, the players will be confident that no surprises will appear on the field of play—the players will be prepared for every eventuality.

For Michael Johnson (1996), the 200- and 400-meter gold medalist in the 1996 Olympic Games, confidence comes from belief in preparation and commitment: "My confidence is knowing that I have probably trained harder than anyone I am going to run against. . . . that translates into the belief that if I am in a race, I am going to win."

Bobby Knight, a well-known American basketball coach, says he looks for players with "the will to prepare to win."

See the Big Picture

Confidence is based on continual achievement, however small, so it is important to maintain progress in all aspects of soccer development. When a player suffers a loss of confidence, it is often because of the failure of one aspect of his or her game. Too much attention to this component can obscure the fact that the player is progressing well in other areas.

Thus it is important for players and coaches to keep the big picture in mind when reviewing progress. My role is to help a player change his or her view of things, a process I call "reframing." Instead of overemphasizing one problem, we create a new picture that includes many aspects of play to be confident about and one area that needs special attention. We can then view this as a challenge, not a problem.

Build a Tick Stepladder

Most research work on goal setting describes the route to high self-esteem and confidence as a "tick stepladder" in which every achievement, no matter how small, is recorded and rewarded. Confidence comes from success and feeling that one can cope with adversity. Achieving small goals regularly, and feeling good about it, is the way to build confidence and coping skills for the big goals.

This approach is useful for players who have suffered a dramatic loss of self-esteem and confidence from deterioration of form or when facing a long recovery from injury. Martin Taylor, a former Derby County goalkeeper of exceptional courage, faced a two-year recovery from a severe injury. With his wife, he planned every step of the way on a large chart on the kitchen wall at home. Every day, every exercise, every hospital visit, every possible sign of progress was given a tick and recorded. Neither would accept any loss of self-esteem, and both were confident that Martin would soon be back playing professional soccer. He returned far sooner than predicted, with greater mental toughness.

Players and coaches should have dreams and visions but should make their ladder one of small and reasonably attainable steps, thus maintaining a constant basis of confidence while moving ever closer to the dream.

Program the Inner Tape

As we move through each day, encountering a stream of varying situations, we constantly talk to ourselves. Our inner tape provides a recording of our state of mind, with those parrots I mentioned helping us determine whether we talk ourselves up or talk ourselves down. Confidence, therefore, is the result of what we say to ourselves about what we think about ourselves.

Players with confidence program their inner tape with positive self-talk, whereas low-confidence players put anxiety into their minds by using negative self-talk. Because we know (see table 2.1) that performance follows attitude and that attitude is based on the confidence a player feels in a given situation, then every player clearly needs training in using positive self-talk and rejecting negative self-talk.

Table 2.2 shows the results of an exercise in self-talk conducted with the England women's senior team. This team had proved more vulnerable to negative self-talk than the men's teams I usually worked with. The exercise, then, was one of opening up the fears and anxieties contained in negative self-talk and then working together to find positive self-talk answers that could replace them.

When I speak to players either individually or as a team, I always try to identify where they are coming from mentally and emotionally. What doubts, fears, and anxieties are playing in their inner tapes at that moment? Of course, my job is to work with the coaches to help the player or team program the tape with different and positive messages. Even in the worst circumstances, success-

TABLE 2.2 CONFIDENCE AND SELF-TALK

Results of an exercise with the England Women's Senior Team, August 1997: changing negative self-talk to positive self-talk

NEGATIVE SELF-TALK	POSITIVE SELF-TALK
I'm not willing to go through this.	I am still willing to pay the price.
I'm not good enough.	Trust the coaches—they selected me.
I won't cope.	I have the experience now to deal with anything.
I'm not ready.	I'm as ready as I'll ever be.
I'm afraid of criticism.	I'll take responsibility for my game and whatever criticism comes.
What about injury?	I always play hard and accept injuries as part of the game.
I'll make mistakes.	I may make mistakes, but I know how to recover.
What if I miss the shot?	I'll get the next one.
What if they score first?	I'll work even harder.
I'll have a bad game and we'll lose.	I only worry about things I can control, so I will play my best and stay in the present.
I don't look good.	I love this kit, and I feel really proud.
We aren't tough enough.	I am happy to walk into the valley of the shadow of death because I know my teammates are the meanest bitches in there!

ful players and teams can find a way to be positive. Players should remember the adage, "What happens to you is not nearly as important as how you react to what happens to you."

Confidence and the Striker Who Can't Score

I have mentioned before the special case of goalkeepers and strikers. For them, reframing is especially important. When Dean Sturridge, the Derby County striker, had a spell when he couldn't score goals, his whole game fell apart. After discussion with Steve McLaren, then the Derby County coach, we asked Dean to observe one of his favorite players—striker Ian Wright, then of Arsenal—and record every contribution Ian made to his team's play. After joint discussion we agreed on five essential elements of a striker's play:

- Scoring goals
- Making goals
- Making forward runs and being available for passes
- Holding the ball up and bringing teammates into play
- Pressuring defenders when they have the ball

We then assessed Dean's present performances on each of these five elements on a score of 1 to 10. Clearly, his marks were low on scoring goals, but he was surprised at the positive scores on other aspects of his play.

The smaller view was that he was not scoring goals—the bigger, more helpful picture was that he was contributing to the team in other ways. Of course, strikers must score goals, but they all have barren periods that they must recover from. Dean's case is an example of how to deal positively with such a problem—maintaining overall confidence and buying time until the next goal comes along, the occurrence that will provide the ultimate confidence boost.

Build a Positive Support Group

Although I urge players to take responsibility for building their own self-concept and confidence, I am aware that every player is influenced, positively or negatively, by the comments received from family and friends, from those who surround him daily.

For all players, especially perhaps for women players who must make difficult choices in order to play soccer, it is essential that the people they share their feelings with—family, partner, teammates, counselor—reinforce their belief in themselves and their motivation to pursue soccer excellence. The background influence of fans and the media may also be important.

Parents, for example, can be part of the problem or part of the solution. Players who receive loving and well-balanced support from their parents are far more likely to overcome the challenge of soccer than those who must try to fulfill parental egos and dreams. Lucky Dan Marino, the great American football quarterback, had a father who used to leave notes hidden for him saying, "I love you—win or fail."

Handling key relationships is a lifestyle skill of the complete player. Part of my counseling always includes how well my players are dealing with the tricky life balance of the demands of soccer and the demands of home. On many occasions, I have been asked to deal with a soccer problem that, upon investigation, turned out to be a problem at home that was spilling over into soccer performance.

In table 2.2 players are urged to ignore the moaners. Confidence is a choice. On one occasion I saw a player take a positive action at halftime in a match by suddenly taking all his clothes and moving to another spot in the dressing room. When I later asked him why he did this, he explained that the new player next to him was moaning nonstop. Although the team was down 0-1, the first player felt the game was still there to be won and he did not want his confidence affected.

Players, coaches, parents, and friends should always remember Coach Vince Lombardi's (1996) belief, "Confidence is contagious. So is lack of confidence."

Screen Out Distractions

Later in this book I will describe mental toughness as remaining positive in the face of adversity. As figure 2.1 illustrates, soccer undoubtedly provides a range of confidence-threatening situations. Bill Parcells (1995), the outstanding American football coach, regards highly the ability of players to ignore things they cannot control while concentrating on the one thing they can control—their minds: "It's easy to get diverted by all the variables outside your control, to let them eat away at your vision and self-confidence. But details will doom you—lose faith in yourself and you will fulfill your own worst prophecy."

Successful players and teams discipline their minds to accept only positive and supportive messages—they actively reject negative interference. Clever coaches work hard to create an environment that limits the possibility of negative interference. Teams at home thus have the advantage because they can more easily control their environment and minimize distractions.

For the last 25 years, Anfield Stadium, the home of Liverpool, has had an awesome reputation for undermining the confidence of visiting teams. To meet this challenge in the 1998–99 season, Derby County set these objectives for their visit to Anfield:

- Beat the environment—minimize all potential negatives.
- Retain all routines and familiarization procedures—consider the match "just another day at the office."
- Beat Liverpool on the field.

By sharing these goals with the players, the coaches raised the players' awareness of potential distractions and insisted on preparing to play in a particular way. Derby beat the environment and produced an excellent performance to defeat Liverpool.

Trust Yourself

Following his first U.S. Open singles championship, Andre Agassi was quoted as saying he won because he finally allowed himself to play well enough to win. This confident player realized that to win big matches he had to trust his skills.

Trust, one step beyond confidence, is a vital part of those outstanding performances when players describe themselves as "being in the zone" or achieving "flow." With complete trust in the ability of their bodies to meet the challenge, players can move into an automatic, virtual no-think situation that allows relaxed excellence.

Coaches can often be heard telling a player to stop thinking so much and just play. They are aware of the benefits a player can get by simply trusting the body to take over and do what is right. Trust is confidence in action.

Coaching to Boost Confidence

Of all the relationships that can influence the player's self-confidence, the one with the coach is the most powerful. The coach, with control of selection, feedback, and so on, has the power to shape the player's attitude positively or negatively.

There was a time when coaches did not concern themselves with players' feelings. They felt that the job was outcome orientated. The goal was to win at any cost, so they considered players expendable along the way. Modern coaches are moving more to player orientation—sharing with players ownership of the challenge and finding ways to boost players' confidence and therefore performance.

For women players all research indicates that the coach is a significant factor in their attitudes to practice and competition—either as a positive or negative influence. Men seem to be more able to stay motivated without positive coach support, but coaches with negative attitudes can still affect confidence.

Clearly, coaches can help players acquire positive attitudes, and therefore confidence, by teaching practice and competition situations in such a way that the player feels motivated and able to meet the challenge. In many ways great coaches are great story tellers. They can inspire and energize players by engaging them in positive dreams of achievement. Coach Pat Riley (1993) gives us an example with his pregame message to the Los Angeles Lakers basketball team before the key playoff game in 1982 against Philadelphia:

> This is our day. Everything has worked perfectly up to this point. We're here, in our city and on our day, to win a championship in front of all our families, our friends, and our fans. There is no pressure. All we have to do is take care of business.

Of course, coaches must criticize a player when his or her performance does not meet the required standards, but in an environment that is mainly positive and supportive, any criticism is relative and should not damage self-esteem and confidence.

Coaches who would like to develop a style that boosts players' self-esteem and confidence might want to check their present strategies with the following guidelines.

Make Learning Fun and Challenging

If young men and women enjoy coming to training, the coach who understands the power of humor can use it as an excellent start to boosting confidence levels. England under-21 coach Sammy Lee, a Liverpudlian with great energy and good humor, always does the warm-up, which sets a positive tone for the session. The head coach, Howard Wilkinson, makes sure each practice ends with a short enjoyable activity so the players leave with smiles on their faces and positive attitudes about their performance.

Treat All Players With Respect

Coach Alex Gibson of Manchester City has the knack of making all his players feel like heroes. When I observe him coach I see that he

- knows and uses every player's name;
- treats each player as a unique individual deserving special attention;
- encourages his boys to express their feelings, ask questions, and come to him with problems, which he listens to carefully; and
- shows patience and understands that sometimes the best thing he can do for a young player is give him some space and time.

Naturally, Alex, qualified both as a teacher and a counselor, is highly respected by the confident young players he produces.

Notice and Reward Good Performance

Confidence is based on achievement. It will always be boosted by observant coaches who look for good performance rather than poor performance and are willing to be vocal and visual in their praise. A positive and clever coach can make every player feel like an achiever but still point out weaknesses. Many coaches achieve this by using the sandwich technique:

- Praise: "Lots of good things there boys . . ."
- Criticism: ". . . but I think we can improve the . . ."
- Praise: ". . . and I know you have the ability to do it."

Coaches will be more likely to notice changes in performance if they have helped each player understand his or her role and how it fits into overall team performance. Coaches who don't work with players individually tend to notice only the mistakes.

Keep Everything in Perspective

I have a view that the world is teeming with good practice coaches but lacks good game coaches. How often do we see confidence built in training destroyed in matches because the coach lacks perspective about what he or she is trying to achieve? An overemotional response to a defeat can destroy confidence that is difficult to rebuild in the following week.

University of Georgetown basketball coach John Thompson provided an excellent example of calm, rational coaching. For the first 36 minutes of every game, he avoided checking the scoreboard, maintaining total focus on helping his players learn to perform well. Only in the last 4 minutes of the game would he become concerned with the outcome, but by then his team had won most of the games by superior performance. A defeat would not be an emotional disaster but a wake-up call to practice a little better and harder.

Rebuilding Confidence at Manchester City

Close to the end of the 1997-98 season, the manager of Manchester City, Joe Royle, and his assistant, Willie Donachie, called me in to help stop the decline of a formerly great club heading toward relegation. Problems of physical, tactical, and technical nature clearly existed, but the coaches felt the most serious concern was a drastic loss of confidence. In an unusual situation, the problem was especially evident in home games, where the team had to contend with a crowd of thirty thousand, which, though wonderfully loyal, could be quite negative and cynical.

Because I wanted to begin by drawing out and recognizing the fear in the situation, I asked the team which day of the week was their worst. After some time, the captain, a fine young man named Kit Symons, displayed the honesty to reply that it was Saturday—match day! Despite the positive nature of the coaches, the situation was defeating the team. They were looking at soccer through the negative window.

My strategy was to

- personally win their confidence and trust,
- acknowledge the fear present as part of the challenge of soccer,
- renew motivation by reviewing why players commit to soccer,
- reframe the state of mind collectively to a bigger and more positive picture,
- redirect attention to what was possible and reasonable to achieve,
- increase energy levels by raising expectations, and
- build their commitment to stay in the game.

The process centered on team talks, individual counseling, supporting and influencing the coaches, being a positive presence at games, and following this 10-step approach:

1. Keeping the big picture—and proper perspective—in front of the players ("What do we need to do to achieve our target?")
2. Getting the players to take "ownership" of realistic targets
3. Being willing to identify and discuss all barriers to achievement
4. Keeping the agenda open and encouraging players to talk, share their fears, and release the tension
5. Defeating anxiety by discussing only factors we could control
6. Being with them on the bad days and helping them move on
7. Introducing the mental skills of relaxation, mistake management, distraction control, and concentration
8. Encouraging leadership from those capable of providing it
9. Comparing our improving mental toughness with that of our opponents and urging the team to stay in the race until the end
10. Being a personal source of inspiration by using stories, case studies, and motivational videos, and by always encouraging humor

(continued)

After winning the final game of the season away from home 5 to 2, the team's fate and relegation were sealed elsewhere, and Manchester City was a point short of survival. Still, I consider my intervention to have substantially rebuilt confidence. Although it was not quite enough in the short term, both the players and the club benefited—as evidenced by their success the following season in winning immediate promotion back to the first division.

Summary

Confidence—the constant belief that the challenges of soccer can be overcome—is the foundation of success. Much of this confidence is programmed internally by players' self-talk. Each player must work constantly to see the positive side of all the situations he or she faces—seeing challenges, not problems. Such an attitude will always stimulate positive emotions, which will produce energy to sustain high levels of performance.

Players can build confidence by making a resolute commitment, by always preparing thoroughly, by rewarding themselves for every little success, by focusing on their objectives, by building a positive social support group, and finally by learning to trust their bodies and the habits they have worked to acquire.

Essential to the building of players' confidence is the philosophy, personality, and style of the coach. All players, especially females, benefit from a player-oriented coach who surrounds them with a positive and supportive culture in which criticism of their performance does not damage self-esteem and confidence.

chapter

3

Self-Control

Discipline of Thought and Emotion

Fire in the belly, ice in the head.

Soccer is a game of both motion and emotion. In the quarterfinals of the 1998 World Cup, England was competing well against Argentina when, in an incident of high emotion, David Beckham lost self-control and was sent from the field. Playing with just 10 men, England went on to lose the game and their dream.

In the final of the same tournament Brazil was expected by many to beat France. On the day of the match, however, their star player, Ronaldo, became ill, and the team prepared to play with his replacement—a well-liked senior player. Just before kickoff Ronaldo recovered, and the decision was made to revert to the original team. Brazil took the field with a team that had changed twice on the day of the match, a coach feeling that he was not in control, and a team that was emotionally washed out. Negative thoughts, the wrong emotional state, and low energy led to a passive performance and a loss in the most important game in world soccer.

Examples like those illustrate the following:

- Soccer can take players on an emotional roller-coaster ride.
- In a single game, players can feel happiness, sadness, fear, anger, surprise, excitement, guilt, and so on.
- Emotions are linked with energy (emotion in Latin means "set in motion") and can build or drain players' energy levels.
- Self-control is one of the most important mental skills in soccer—any loss of control will disrupt all aspects of play.

Changes in the nature of soccer have also defined the increasing importance of self-control. In the days when soccer was primarily considered a physically intimidating encounter—a war without weapons—coaches created high emotion and expected players to lose control occasionally. Changes in rules and tactics have made soccer more strategic—perhaps more like basketball. Coaches now require players who can demonstrate patience, discipline, and self-control.

The lesson to be learned from the failure of Brazil is that central to winning is the ability of each player, the team, and the coach to create a stable emotional state before the game and maintain it for 90 minutes. Players and teams who let their mental and emotional state disrupt their physical, technical, and tactical prowess will always underachieve.

Figure 3.1 shows the process players should use to achieve good self-control:

1. The player's state of mind—how he or she perceives the challenge of soccer—must be positive, confident, and relaxed.
2. The player will then be prepared with positive emotions.
3. Potentially stressful incidents will not undermine the player's self-control.
4. Such self-control will allow the player's physical ability to flourish.
5. Calm and successful coping strategies will provide feedback and reinforce the player's positive state of mind.

Loehr and McLaughlin (1990) emphasize the link between state of mind, emotions, and the supply of energy. They differentiate between high positive energy (energy without tension), the ideal state for self-controlled performance, and high negative energy (energy with tension), a dangerous state in which control is easily

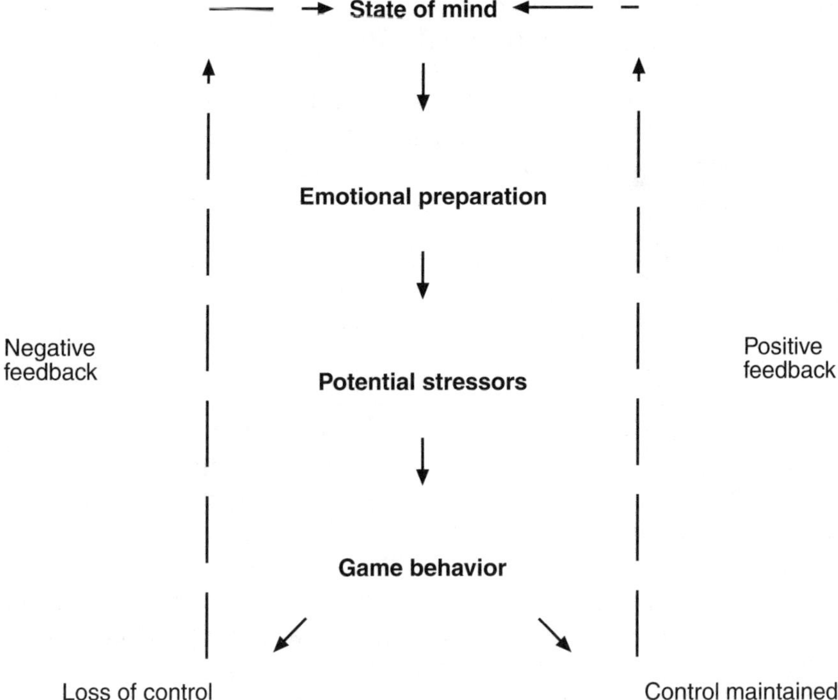

Figure 3.1 The process of self-control.

and quickly lost. Clearly, David Beckham moved instantly from high positive energy to high negative energy. Provocation created an attitude change with a corresponding surge of anger that resulted in his loss of self-control and dismissal.

Much of my work with players and teams centers on shaping the attitudes and emotions that can create and maintain a state of high positive energy. By starting with a positive attitude and knowing how to apply pertinent coping strategies, the player should be able to ride the emotional roller coaster of soccer without loss of control.

Emotional Intelligence

Soccer will always be an emotional experience for players, either positive or negative. The problem is not with emotionality but with the appropriateness of the emotions created and their expression.

Players who cannot control their emotions will find themselves fighting inner battles, (for example, guilt), that sabotage their ability for focused work and clear thought. Emotion and skill execution go hand in hand.

Bill Parcells (1995) sums up the problem in American football:

> A lot of kids we get nowadays have grown up macho. They can't take a dirty look, a harsh word, and they definitely can't take a slap on the back of the head from some cheap-shot artist on the other team.
>
> But mature players will absorb these in their stride, even when they are out-and-out flagrant. I tell my players to put their emotions on hold—to stoneface their opponent. If he knows what you're thinking he has an advantage.

The question then is how to handle emotions with intelligence, enhancing and energizing performance rather than deenergizing and disrupting it. Just as there is a sport intelligence that accelerates physical and technical learning, so too there is an emotional intelligence that embraces the skills of self-control.

Self-control, then, requires the intelligence to manage yourself and those around you in emotionally charged situations. Orlick (1986) defines self-control as "the ability to perform well under a variety of stress-producing circumstances."

Table 3.1 allows you to rate yourself and your team on how well you are managing your self-control, and table 3.2 identifies five key stressors soccer players face and the appropriate emotionally intelligent response.

TABLE 3.1 A CHECKLIST FOR "EMOTIONAL INTELLIGENCE"

Assess yourself, and then your team, against the criteria below

	A	S	N
Prepares emotionally for games			
Never under- or over-aroused			
Able to handle the big game			
Maintains self-belief with positive talk			
Persists in the face of frustration			
Adapts easily to any situation			
Copes calmly with stress			
Can be relied upon in critical moments			
Deals with other people in a mature, positive manner			
Accepts accountability for actions—never seeks excuses			
Regardless of circumstances, can be trusted			

Key

A - Always

S - Sometimes

N - Never

TABLE 3.2 SOCCER STRESSORS AND RESPONSES

KEY STRESSOR	EMOTIONALLY INTELLIGENT RESPONSE
Change	The life of a soccer player is one of almost constant change. Instead of feeling alarm, players must convert change into a new challenge and respond in a positive manner.
Fear	Players should understand that fear is a survival mechanism common to all people. Fear of failure helps prevent complacency. Players must learn to manage it constructively, providing the energy to meet the challenge of performance.
Distractions	The bigger the game, the bigger the sideshow. Players must manage this assault on their emotions and have the mental strength to get past distractions. They should strive to build a reputation of being able to play well anywhere, anytime, and in any conditions.
Guilt	Mistakes in soccer are usually followed by a surge of guilt and energy that players often use negatively, making one mistake into two. Players have to acknowledge that they will make mistakes in the game. They must accept each mistake as it happens, learn to let go of the guilt, and recover a positive attitude.
Anger	Anger is part of players' arousal mechanism in preparing to compete. Players can use the mobilized energy positively for assertive and expressive play, or they can use it negatively and lose control. We ask England players to be like good boxers—angry but never losing their temper.

A 12-Step Strategy for Achieving Self-Control

Like confidence, self-control is an option that players can choose. Players must decide to take responsibility for their actions and not seek excuses. When we go through a difficult period at Derby County, I remind the players that although they cannot control much of what is happening around them, they can choose how they respond.

Self-control strategies are based on the relationship between thought and emotion. We know that our state of mind influences our emotions, which in turn energizes our performance. So if we wish to improve our performance by controlling our emotions we must change our thinking.

I offer a 12-step strategy to help players learn the skill and discipline of self-control, but players should only take the steps they feel are right for them. Players can begin the process only when they take full responsibility for their actions.

1. Awareness—analyze when loss of control has occurred in the past—why, when, and where on the soccer field. Identify your personal weak spots.

2. Understanding—realize why your thinking changed and how it caused you to lose emotional balance.

3. Differences—recall when you did not lose control and when you did in similar circumstances. What were the differences in your attitudes, emotions, and behavior?

4. Problem—try to pinpoint the problem. For example, is it the sudden guilt of letting your team down?

5. Belief—raise the expectations you have for yourself and include self-control as one of your virtues. You can change!

6. Reinforcement—behavior change is accelerated by reinforcement, so you and your support group should reward improved behavior on the way to permanent change.

7. Goals—set yourself a series of small goals, perhaps with the agreement of your coach, that will lead you along the route to change.

8. Techniques—build a series of behavioral techniques for maintaining composure, that is, if such and such happens, then I will do this (walk away from the incident, for example).

9. Plan—pursue your goals in a planned, systematic way, selecting a personal blend of techniques from those suggested in this chapter.

10. Progress—improvement comes in a series of ups and downs, so be patient.

11. Setbacks—accept that setbacks will happen from time to time, forgive yourself, and become even stronger.

12. Remembrance—recall frequently why you are doing this and what the future will be if you don't change.

Techniques to Improve Self-Control

By following certain guidelines, you can improve self-control. The following techniques will be useful.

Be Prepared

Most situations when a player might lose control can be anticipated and prepared for—by the player alone, with the coach, or with the team psychologist. By mentally playing the match beforehand, the player can tune in to the possible stressors and prepare appropriate responses to ensure control.

An experienced coach or sports psychologist can help the player understand the link between thoughts, feelings, and actions. They can review previous incidents—wherever possible I use videotape for this—and examine differences between successful and unsuccessful self-control. The player must look not only at behavioral performance but also at emotional performance. The player should try to recall what he or she was feeling during the particular incident. The player must finish such a review with a "solution bank"—a set of solutions to predictable problem areas in the form "if that happens, then I will do this."

In my first match as sports psychologist to the England under-18 team, I was taken by surprise early in the game when our star player was sent off after reacting to some close and bruising marking. I have always regretted not preparing him for a situation when it was likely that defenders would give him special, and provocative, attention. We might have developed a mind-set for him to accept the relentless attention and use it to create space for his teammates, knowing that by showing patience and self-control early in the game, he would later have chances as defenders grew tired of chasing him.

Be Relaxed

The ideal performance state for a soccer player is that of "relaxed readiness"—possessing energy without tension. This state allows players to stay calm, loose, and responsive to the pressures of the game. Relaxation techniques can help players control their thinking so they can trigger emotions that remove unnecessary tension and conserve energy. Anxiety is often described as "information that won't go away." Relaxation, the clearing of the mind, gives the player an effective way of dealing with it and moving toward relaxed readiness. Botterill and Patrick (1996) emphasize these psychological benefits:

> It's a great time to park [set aside] any distracting or dysfunctional thoughts or cues and refocus on performance or situationally relevant cues instead. Negative thoughts can be parked or dispersed along with any tension as you exhale and refocus on your body responding more effectively.

Emotions are considered the windows of our physiology, and relaxation prepares players for the critical incidents in soccer when positive thinking, body control, and energy control are part of the solution.

Relaxation techniques players can use include

- stretching,
- breathing control,
- arousal management (music, video),
- massage, and
- visualization.

Players who wish to develop relaxation skills should organize a quiet place with a comfortable seat. They should select something to focus on, allow a passive attitude to develop, and seek to enjoy the state of nothingness. Players should try various techniques until they find one that is agreeable and then practice it so it becomes a tool they can go to instantly in moments of stress.

Develop Performance Routines

If emotions follow our thoughts then clearly any behavioral routines that help control our thinking will lead to better emotional self-control.

When preparing to play, all soccer players are subjected to positive and negative thinking, but attitude is a choice. The mentally strong player will allow only positive thoughts to predominate. Players should develop an active behavioral routine that keeps them busy, is familiar and comforting, and has connection to positive thoughts and emotions.

When building his self-belief, Lee Carsley (see the introduction) was most vulnerable to doubt immediately before a game. We developed a reminder card that reaffirmed positive messages and anchored Lee's mind to a positive and assertive state:

- Be confident
- Know my job
- Breathe deeply—stay composed
- Do simple things well
- Feel good—smile
- Win my battles
- Relax and enjoy myself
- Stay strong for 90 minutes
- Seize the day—have no regrets

At some stage before the game Lee would find a quiet spot and read the card several times, ensuring that these were the last thoughts in his mind before playing.

Players may consider several other performance routines.

Positive Self-Talk

Players should discipline themselves to allow only positive self-talk.

Physical Reminders

Players might use a signal, for example, a clap of the hands, to restore positive thinking when they realize they have slipped into the negative. Jacob Laursen, a Danish international who is extremely strong mentally, ends his pregame warm-up with 10 defensive headers and then one volley clearance, which propels him into a confident and focused mental state.

Modeling

When a player is having problems with self-identity, a way to create a more positive attitude is to model a player he or she admires. Mart Poom, the Estonian national goalkeeper, models himself on the great Danish goalkeeper, Peter Schmeichel. When Poom suffers a period of doubt he simply asks, "What would Peter do?" and gains the direction and strength to move on.

Powerful and Positive Visual Messages

Generally, players love to look at soccer images. Photographs, artwork, or video films can capture their imagination at vital times. When England under-18 had to beat Russia to stay in the European championship, I asked the captain, Jonathan Woodgate, what kind of pregame meeting would most benefit our team. Jonathan recommended that we meet to watch again the powerful motivational video "The Winner Takes It All." We did and we won!

The use of visual images is now commonplace at Derby. We use them to arouse players, help them relax, or build their focus. For example, we have found that playing the highlights film on the team bus just before arriving at an away stadium can help distract players from a hostile environment and build positive arousal.

- Visualization—a process in which the player visualizes the desired performance to banish negative thoughts (see chapter 5).

• Control distractions—if anxiety is information that won't go away, then the greatest danger to players' self-control are internal or external distracting messages that destroy attention and trigger negative emotional response.

Soccer is a game of read and react, with players reading the ever-changing performance situation and choosing and executing the correct response. Successful players excel at both reading the game and knowing what information to ignore—they are unlikely to be distracted.

England 4, Distractions 0

At an international fixture in Yugoslavia, it became clear that the team could be more affected by distractions–transport, food, hotel, training facilities, boredom, an awful pitch, and so on–than the opposition. I approached this challenge using the traffic-light metaphor suggested by Ravizza and Hanson (1995) and the following strategy:

- Players and staff brainstormed all possible distractions so we would know what was coming.
- We posted the list and ticked them off when they occurred, which proved to be an amusing game rather than an irritation.
- I asked the group if distractions could beat us. "No!" they answered.
- I then asked what color would best describe our self-control if we allowed distractions to beat us. They replied that we would see red.
- If we stayed in perfect control and progressed smoothly, then we would see green.
- Having recognized the traffic-light metaphor, I asked how a player goes from green to red–through amber, of course.
- We then agreed that amber was the moment of decision, the time when we would either return to green or go on to red.
- After discussion we listed the techniques that would help us in the moments when we hovered in amber:
    - Breathe deep and relax.

(continued)

- Walk away to buy some time.
- Release the tension—clap hands, stretch, and so on.
- Recognize that a teammate needs help. The group de cided that we would have a standard call, "Stay in the green." At one stage in the game Lee Matthews was being severely provoked when his captain, Matthew Upson, yelled to him, "Lee, stay in the green." Lee smiled, relaxed, and did not go into the red.
- Park it until later. If a distraction occurs that we might have to deal with, but not now, we immediately park it to one side until, say, halftime.
- Win the game. Remember that distractions help you lose.

This case study had a happy ending as England won 4-0 in appalling conditions and under a great deal of provocation. Because the players were prepared for distractions and the team and staff had committed to "staying in the green," the level of self-control was outstanding. The final message in the changing room was England 4, Distractions 0.

Mistake Management

When I observe a soccer game I am probably the only person in the stadium not watching the ball. I watch my team's players, especially their behavior after they have made a mistake. Nothing tests a player's self-control more than making a clear mistake—goalkeepers and strikers are especially vulnerable—in front of thirty thousand people.

If I have done my work properly, the player will have a recovery strategy to deal with the dangers of an emotional surge of guilt, which may cause the player either to become passive and hide or to overreact and compound the first mistake into an even worse second one. Mistakes are part of the game, so planning for mistakes is not negative thinking but positive preparation.

Failure to teach mistake management leaves players without the tools they need to maintain control and prevent a deterioration in performance. Players often receive yellow and red cards because they overreact to mistakes. Coaches all too often concentrate on punishing the mistakes rather than working with the player on potential corrections.

Anger Management

In a highly competitive and physically challenging game like soccer, a certain amount of anger will always be present. Both coaches and players often induce anger toward the opposition, which creates an emotional surge that in people more accustomed to fight than flight produces a state of high energy.

But anger can hinder performance as well as help it. Unless players learn to manage anger, it can produce several negative effects:

- Loss of focus—becoming blind with anger
- Loss of control to the opponent—losing focus and giving them chances
- Loss of productive play—wasting valuable time to recover
- Loss of trust by the coach
- Loss of fun and friendship—soccer becoming a battle

Role of the Coach

Coaches must understand that players must maintain emotional control in order to perform to their physical and technical potential. Emotional readiness must be regarded as part of overall individual and team preparation to play, as illustrated by figure 3.2.

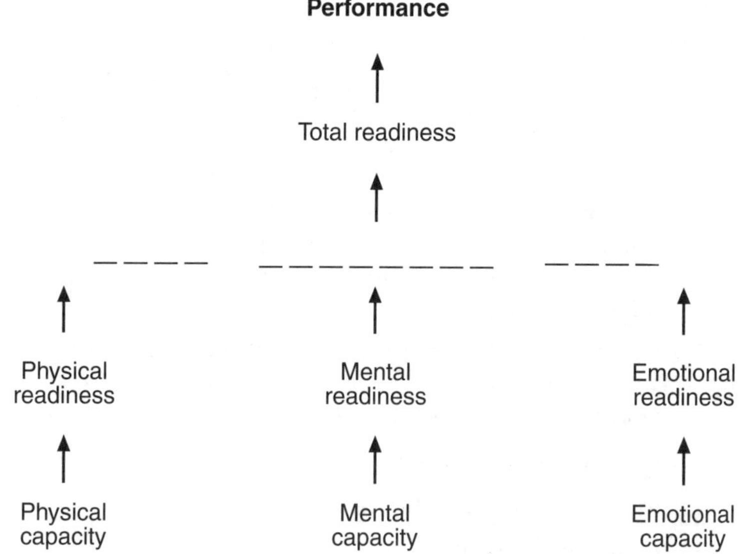

Figure 3.2 Balanced preparation to play.

Treat setbacks as part of the journey.

The coach must therefore plan a program that shapes and reinforces positive thinking by the players, creating an emotional state that energizes the team to begin the game in a state of relaxed readiness. The coach cannot create a winning team unless he or she is willing to deal with and influence the emotional state of the team. As one of England's senior coaches, Colin Murphy, puts it, "No coach is likely to have a team of 'Steady Eddies'—it is how he deals with the 'Fiery Freds' or the 'Demon Daves' that will determine the success of his team."

We emphasize the importance of emotional preparation when preparing the England under-21 team by always considering the following aspects of our coaching program:

- Are they physically ready?
- Are they technically ready?
- Are they mentally ready?
- Are they emotionally ready?

Gary Learns Not to Turn One Mistake Into Two

To all outward appearances, Gary Rowett was a capable and composed defender for Derby County. In fact, Gary was sensitive and became so troubled when he made mistakes that he lost confidence and performed well below his potential.

My first step was to monitor Gary's performance, with special attention to mistakes and subsequent behavior changes. Every time Gary was directly involved I would award him a tick for a successful contribution and a cross for a mistake. After six games, we reviewed the pattern to see what it revealed about Gary's mental state during a match:

- He always started well.
- Inevitably he would make one or two mistakes.
- The mistakes would begin to affect his confidence and control.
- Mistakes would then come in clusters.
- Mistakes might even occur in the vital defensive third of the pitch.

We solved most of the problem simply by raising Gary's awareness—by letting him see his performance, the pattern of mistakes, in visual form. We could link his thinking and feelings after mistakes to the resulting pattern of behavior. He immediately agreed to take responsibility for change by minimizing mistakes and, more important, by rationalizing and improving his self-control on those that would still occur. We settled on two important actions:

1. Gary would adopt a no-risk approach to any ball in the defensive third of the pitch, markedly reducing any chance of mistakes there.

2. After a mistake occurred, Gary's route back to confidence and emotional stability would be to make sure that his next touch of the ball was positive. He would select a safe option, and success with that touch would act as a release from the first mistake. He would then forget the mistake, and no longer would mistakes come in clusters.

This proved to be successful mistake management. Gary has become a more mature and trustworthy defender.

In considering the last question, the lessons of this chapter for coaches are these:

- Improve players' awareness of the importance of being emotionally ready to perform.
- Understand that by shaping the thinking of players, you will influence their emotional states.
- When the team is not performing, examine the links between state of mind, emotions, and energy levels.
- Give players techniques for building self-control. If possible use a sports psychologist.
- Be patient with younger players.
- Reinforce and reward players who demonstrate the intelligence to manage themselves emotionally.
- Use video, music, and other forms of communication to influence players' mental and emotional states.
- Prepare an emotional game plan that reviews the upcoming game and sensitizes the team to likely emotional flash points.
- Be sensitive to the nature and delivery of pregame, halftime, and postgame team talks—consider the likely emotional impact on players.
- Manage the game environment carefully to minimize distractions and avoid surprises on game day.

Finally, coaches should reflect on their own management of emotions. After observing a youth team that was going through a difficult time, I asked permission to video a game. I concentrated my taping on the uncontrolled and negative performance of the coaches. When I replayed the video to them, they were stunned and embarrassed. Apologies followed, and everything changed from that point. The coaches learned the lesson that self-control begins with them, and they became supportive observers and analysts.

Anger Control Saves a Young Player

A major club referred a young player to me—a player of exceptional physical ability who had no control over his anger. His abuse of himself, teammates, opponents, and referees caused the coaches to lose all trust in him. I was the last stop before the club would release him. Fortunately, the young man wanted to change, and we quickly identified a process he felt comfortable with:

- By frank discussion, supported by video evidence, we identified the triggers that caused his anger.
- We agreed on a list of coping reactions that he might adopt when those triggers occurred in the future. If he became angry, he would
  - focus on breathing,
  - repeat the word "relax,"
  - walk away,
  - increase positive self-talk,
  - project calm body language, and
  - visualize his role model.
- We agreed to be patient and use any setbacks as a chance to review and confirm our strategy. At the same time I persuaded the coaches to show more patience—sometimes the most important factor in dealing with young players—and to recognize and reinforce any behavior changes they observed.

Once the player became more concerned with showing control than defending his ego, the coping strategies took effect and he began to earn the trust of the coaches. Quick-fix solutions do not exist, and I warned both the player and his coaches that occasional lapses might occur. But for the time being, the player showed enough improvement that the club retained him and gave him more time to change his behavior.

Summary

A coach must know whether he or she can trust a player. The modern player may well have more issues to deal with off the pitch than on it. Most players will need a great deal of help to achieve the stable state needed for success on the emotional roller coaster of soccer.

Players and coaches must pay more attention to developing emotional readiness to play. Self-control must be emphasized as a characteristic of excellence. The emotional game plan must include steps to achieve the confident state of mind that will lead to a positive emotional state and high energy levels. Coaches must teach management of mistakes and anger because both can instantly destroy self-control.

The coach-player and coach-team relationships are important to emotional stability, so the coach must become both an effective, sensitive communicator and a powerful role model.

chapter 4

Concentration

Direction and Intensity of Attention

© Erza O. Shaw/ALLSPORT

Ninety-nine percent concentration equals 100 percent failure.

The European club championship final of 1999 lasted for 93 minutes. As the game entered the 90th minute, Bayern Munich was up 1-0, and their players had clearly begun to celebrate a great victory. One player was even waving to a friend in the crowd!

Manchester United, still fully focused, seized on that lapse of concentration and scored two goals in the final three minutes to achieve a remarkable comeback. For Bayern it was truly a case of 99 percent concentration not being enough in a major final.

This book emphasizes that performance follows attitude. We have already examined the importance of confidence and self-control in players' attitude. Concentration—being able to focus attention on one aspect of performance for the time necessary to be successful—is the third major element of attitude.

Years ago, the two essential strategic principles of soccer—ball movement and player movement—were limited by a combination of poor technique, a heavy ball, and slow pitches. Today's game is different; a goalkeeper's pass can initiate a goal scored in less than four seconds.

Players must now deal with a transitional game of speed and variation and be able to overcome a continual unfolding of problems. Concentration skills are vital if players are to meet the challenge of a complex, fast-moving game that offers many negative distractions.

Players who cannot maintain concentration are subject to several elements that can undermine good performance including:

1. loss of focus—failure to recognize and attend to changes in the pattern of the game, and
2. loss of intensity—decline in the power of focus through, for example
    - complacency—the overconfidence of success,
    - choking—the fear of failure or success, and
    - fatigue—the decline of energy available.

Rudd Gullit, the former Dutch national team player, once remarked that a 90-minute game of soccer would often be decided by one moment. Every game will contain significant situations when the player defines the moment or the moment defines the player. A lapse of concentration often determines that moment. Part of shaping players' attitudes toward a mentally tough performance is helping them become aware of, and prepare for, defining moments.

Concentration Brings Order to Chaos

Players must learn to recognize and make sense of the flow of the game—the continuous stream of images as players and the ball constantly change positions. Each player, relative to his or her position, must learn to focus attention on situations developing within his or her control while at the same time ignoring situations that are either less important or beyond control.

Doing this is not easy. For some players, it proves to be the weakness that prevents progress, but anyone can develop the ability. Concentration is a habit, not a talent, and it requires motivation and constant practice.

Players will find themselves in two main situations on the field that demand different levels of concentration:

1. Prime responsibility—the action of the game is in the player's area of the pitch and he or she has responsibility for doing a job to help the team. The player must therefore concentrate totally.
2. Support responsibility—the action is away from the player and he or she should be ready to provide support if needed. The player can relax from total concentration.

It might help players to think of their concentration like the action of a flashlight. For prime responsibility, the player must set the flashlight on a narrow beam (specific focus) with powerful intensity (high energy). This, of course, consumes considerable energy—for the light and the player—so when the action moves away the player may switch the light to a much wider beam. The player stays informed and ready but reduces intensity to recover and conserve energy.

If a player can understand the concept of concentration—switching on to a narrow focus with high intensity and then smoothly switching off to a wider view with low intensity—then he or she can obtain rest when possible, begin to reduce the number of mental lapses, and start winning the defining moments.

Eric Steele, goalkeeping coach at Derby, constantly emphasizes that concentration is vital for a goalkeeper. Figure 4.1 illustrates the "funnel of attention," showing prime and support responsibilities and when and where the keeper must switch on and switch off.

When the ball is in position 1—the opponents' half of the field, the goalkeeper is in support responsibility, switching off into

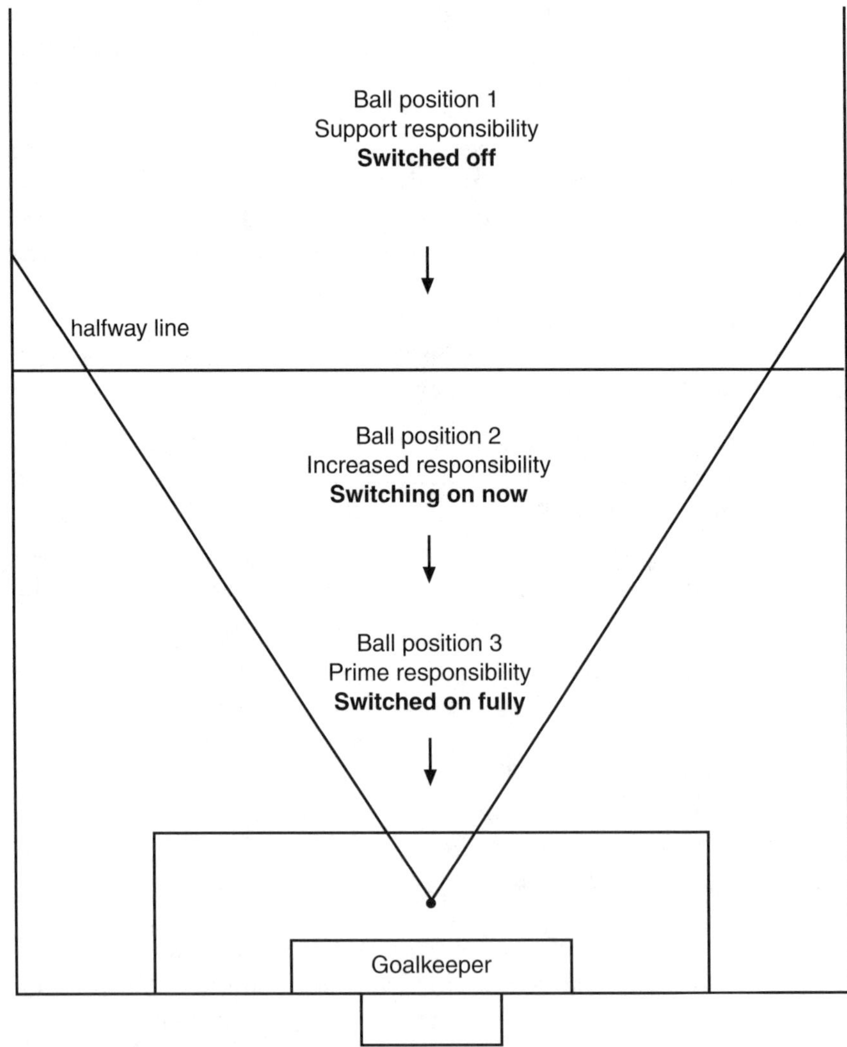

Figure 4.1 The goalkeeper's funnel of attention.

relaxed awareness and taking the opportunity to recover energy.

As the ball moves to position 2, responsibility increases. The goalkeeper must switch on and begin to focus on the developing pattern of play.

When the ball reaches position 3, shooting distance, the goalkeeper has prime responsibility and switches on to total focus and total intensity. Nothing should distract the keeper here.

So the goalkeeper demonstrates the basis of concentration—changing from narrow, focused attention when attack threatens to wide, relaxed, but aware attention when attack is not imminent.

Players must learn, by reviewing the pattern of the game, when they should switch on and when they can safely switch off. They must also be aware of the danger of allowing their inner thoughts and feelings to disrupt this process.

Feelings of frustration, anger, or fatigue can interfere with the process of concentration. The player can find himself or herself paying more attention to an inner world than the outer world of the game. Vince Lombardi (1996) said, "Fatigue makes cowards of us all," causing us to concentrate on what we want, rest, rather than what the game is demanding from us.

Quality Practice Is Essential

Learning to manage focus and intensity begins in training. Only later can players transfer it to competition. Players must accept the link between training and competition and be willing to train at an intensity that will make transfer possible. It is foolish to train at 60 percent intensity and hope that it will transfer to 100 percent on game day—how you practice is how you play!

Some years ago I watched an excellent coach work with young players. He organized his practice in a 60-by-40 meter space but kept one ball for each player spaced along one touch line. Occasionally he would break off from his main practice by having each boy take one ball from the touch line, dribble down the field and back, replace the ball, and rejoin him. The coach explained that this was his way of ensuring quality practice. When mistakes occurred, alerting him to a loss of focus and intensity, he sent the boys off on their relaxed dribble. When they returned he could recover their intensity and the quality of practice.

Jim Taylor (1998) defined four laws of training to achieve focus and intensity:

Law 1: The purpose of training is to develop effective technical, tactical, and mental skills and habits.

Law 2: Whatever players need to do in competition, they must first do in training.

Law 3: Prime training (being able to train at a consistently high level throughout a training session) requires clear purpose and prime focus and intensity.

Law 4: Consistent training leads to consistent competitive performance.

Table 4.1 identifies how to develop focus skills (the ability to pay attention to the task at hand) and intensity skills (the power and length of that attention) by emphasizing certain aspects of training.

TABLE 4.1 DEVELOPING FOCUS AND INTENSITY IN TRAINING

Ways to develop focus skills	
Conducting realistic and demanding practice	Assessing the quality of practice
Preparing and teaching	Knowing what to focus on
Knowing when to relax the focus	Recognizing defining moments
Managing mistakes without loss of focus	Recovering focus after mental lapses
Using key words or physical action to activate focus	Using team calls that activate focus
Punishing loss of focus	Rewarding and reinforcing good focus
Ways to develop intensity	
Using pretraining relaxation to build energy	Building fitness levels to accommodate high intensity
Establishing arousal control	Using positive self-talk and being committed
Being prepared for and avoiding distractions	Concentrating on what can be controlled and ignoring the uncontrollables
Knowing when to move between active focus, semiactive focus, and relaxed focus	Recognizing when key moments require extra intensity and being able to switch on

Building Concentration

You can use several strategies to build concentration.

Know Your Own Style

It is important for each player to prepare a concentration routine that is both effective and comfortable. Some players favor a routine that they complete in isolation with complete control over the situation. Others prefer a routine that allows them to continue interacting with the world around them, and be stimulated, in fact, by the effect of others.

Players should select a concentration method by personal preference and develop a routine and style they can go to when necessary. The mental skills of focus and intensity are no different from physical techniques—they will become habits, and therefore automatic, only through repetition.

Such mental habits help players deal with stress situations when their concentration could easily waver. The ideal performance state is often described as being automatic. Players simply release, with trust, the physical and mental habits established in practice.

Develop a Transition Zone

Players come to practice and competition from particular home and lifestyle backgrounds. Increasingly, I have noticed that players carry concentration problems from one role to another. John Wooden (1972) summed up the focus and intensity that individuals need to switch on to move into the role of being a player: “When you come to practice you cease to exist as an individual—you’re part of a team.”

Players and clubs may find the need for a transition zone that blocks contamination and distractions from passing from one phase of life to another. This can help players focus on one thing at a time, encouraging them to switch on when they come to soccer and switch off when they return home.

Manchester United effects this transition by starting each day with the “box”—a circle of players who keep possession of the ball from two defenders in the middle. As each player arrives on the field to start practice, they receive the yellow bib to become a defender. When this well-established routine has switched on all the players, the coach knows they are focused and ready to practice with quality.

Derby County, on the other hand, has created a transitional-zone meeting room where players report to start their day. A combination of relaxation chairs, music, general and soccer specific videos, and attitude-programming short talks all act to effect a transition in the players' minds from personal life to club and professional responsibilities, which improves their ability to concentrate and produce quality practice.

Players who wish to manage this transition individually should consider techniques such as listening to tapes in the car, reading reminder cards with focus messages, or taking a short walk somewhere near practice where they can enter the cocoon of concentration and ready themselves to perform.

Set Goals

It is important that players always keep at the front of their minds what they want from each practice or game. A clear set of goals allows players to

- focus on priorities,
- begin to eliminate distractions, and
- start to create the discipline and intensity they need to achieve.

Although players may create their own set of goals to help them improve concentration, coaches can help by giving each practice a clear purpose and each game a specific game plan in which players have identifiable roles. If a player knows exactly what his or her targets are at practice and in games, it is far easier to build and develop good concentration routines.

Relax and Conserve Energy

Maintaining concentration is fatiguing, yet players must come to play with maximum energy. Returning to our flashlight metaphor, we must be sure that the battery is fully charged. Relaxation and the conservation of energy play an important part in this.

Lou Holtz (1989), the great American football coach, insisted that his players at Notre Dame stay together the night before a game when he personally conducted a one-and-a-half-hour relaxation class.

I have found players and coaches to be disciplined about work habits but not about relaxation. They would benefit from learning relaxation procedures they could feel comfortable with.

Always Be Prepared

A player building a concentration routine needs to know as much as possible about what he or she will definitely have to do in the game and what he or she might have to do in the game. The player can then begin creating priorities for focus and a solution bank that contains effective responses to particular circumstances.

Several items can help the player prepare focus and intensity:

- Knowing his or her job. Each player should agree with the coach on a clear "job description."
- Understanding the roles and responsibilities of the position within the team's tactical formation.
- Knowing the opponent. An experienced player who knows the opponent will think through their strengths and weaknesses and identify priorities for concentration.
- Having a practice plan. Coaches should conduct practice drills that provide both physical and mental exercise by clearly communicating to players where and when to apply focus and intensity.
- Having a game plan. If coaches are prepared with a plan for winning and an expectation of what will happen, players will have a framework for building their own concentration plan.

From this information base, players may visualize the game—bringing reality forward in the mind—and build their personal concentration plan. This, of course, will have to fit the team consensus on how the players prepare and build focus and intensity as a group. Table 4.2 shows what the England under-18 team developed as their way of preparing for international matches.

Regulate Your State of Arousal

Players must learn to check and regulate their state of arousal—too much and they may be out of control emotionally and wasting energy, too little and they may not be able to produce the required intensity of concentration and effort.

TABLE 4.2 PREPARING FOR OPTIMUM PERFORMANCE

England under-18 team, June 1998: Team view / response

The day before we should:	• Be positive and relaxed • Have a short practice—set plays • Be professional re: lifestyle • Eat and sleep well • Visualize our role/responsiblities
On game day it's best if we:	• Become focused on winning • Avoid all distractions • Eat/drink/rest correctly • Practice positive self-talk • Turn up tuned in—and on time

When we reach the changing room on game day:

We must concentrate on:	Other players can help by:	We like it best when the coaches:
• Building energy/arousal	• Positive talk/spirit	• Talk positively
• Narrowing concentration	• Respecting individual	• Give personal reminders
• Self-preparation—physical	• Communicating	• Give key team reminders
• Self-preparation—mental	• Positive reminders	• Do not talk too much
• Rehearsing our job	• Good humor	• Show no fear

The warm-up will only work if:	• Everyone contributes • Everyone focuses • There are game-related reminders • It is enjoyable • It is not rushed—feeling comfortable

In the changing room immediately before the game:

The atmosphere must be:	We must concentrate on:	We must not think about:
• Togetherness	• Building arousal	• Anything negative
• Serious but relaxed	• Our jobs	• The last game
• Aggressive with control	• Helping the team	• Mistakes
• Confident	• Getting switched on	• Injuries
• Professional	• Feeling ready	• Defeat

If we can do this our game will be like this:	• Enthusiastic • Focused • Committed • Relaxed • Energetic • Together • Aggressive • Bold

Depending on their state of mind, players may either need to (a) psych themselves up with physical activation, high-energy thinking, talking themselves up, motivational music or videos, and so on, or (b) calm themselves down by slow breathing, slowing the pace, performing relaxation exercises, smiling, and so on.

Concentrating in the Game

Many things happen in soccer that can destroy concentration. This will not occur, however, if the player has mental discipline and can control his or her thinking in moments of crisis. Several tools can help the player develop the mental discipline of thought control in the game.

Managing Anxiety

Every player feels anxiety, but successful players learn how to manage it. When anxiety strikes during a game, often after a mistake, a useful recovery process is to

- recover breathing control,
- ease the tension out of the body,
- talk yourself back into the positive,
- let the fear go, and
- review your goals and reactivate yourself toward achievement.

Developing Performance Routines

The bigger the game, the more important good performance habits will be. If players have paid the price over the years of practice, they will have a memory bank of performance routines to deal with any situation. I once heard a ballet dancer explain how she worked hard on her steps from Monday to Friday so she could forget them when the music began for the Saturday show. Performing automatically like this produces a no-think situation—the ultimate thought control.

Using Performance Cues

Players will occasionally suffer mental lapses during a game, especially when fatigued, and will often use shouts or quick physical actions to shake themselves back into focus. Teammates often do this for each other with a team call that urges better concentration and effort.

Brian Miller (1997) describes how a premier rugby league team defending their try line would call "red zone" to heighten concentration, emphasize low-risk tactics, and activate determined tackling.

Controlling Distractions

Loss of concentration in games is often due to a lack of mental discipline in dealing with distractions. Many likely distractions can be anticipated and prepared for. For example, when playing a match away from home, players who are well-prepared by their coaches will be able to shut out the taunting of the home crowd. To improve their chances of winning, players should focus only on what they can control rather than diverting focus and energy to elements they cannot control—notably referees and opponents.

Staying in the Now

Total focus means being locked into the here and now, but players may lapse mentally and go into the past, often because of worry and guilt about an earlier mistake, or into the future, perhaps because the mind begins to anticipate the outcome.

Billie Jean King, in an article for the *Sunday Times* (7 February 1994) describes how she helped Martina Navratilova focus for the Wimbledon tennis final:

> All you can do is get her in the NOW. You know when you are in that zone the ball becomes a basketball and time slows down. You have to be with the ball in the NOW. Don't slip into the past or the future. If she is dreaming (past or future) I bring her back into the NOW—last match I asked her to describe the wallpaper in the changing room. The trick is teaching her to do it for herself in the game.

Players, therefore, must focus on the process, not the outcome, believing that if they take care of the present by concentrating on each situation as it unfolds and responding well, then the outcome will take care of itself.

Each player must be willing to do his or her part in developing a successful team.

Some years ago I helped Joe Royle, the former manager of Oldham Athletic, because his team consistently choked when in sight of promotion. My advice was based on the sport of rowing:

> Remember the rower who cannot see the finishing line . . . and knows he can be first only if he continues to concentrate on the power, efficiency and effectiveness of each movement that carries him away from his opponent and towards the line.

Beating Fatigue

The great destroyer of concentration in games is fatigue—physical, mental, or both—so players must work constantly on their fitness and understand how to pace a game to conserve energy when they can. When England teams play abroad in hot climates, we urge them to work smarter, not harder.

To concentrate with efficiency, players must maintain awareness and recognize game situations when they can switch concentration between total focus, semifocus, and relaxed focus.

Players and teams who do not learn this skill often pay the price toward the end of each half when fatigue hits and mental lapses occur. In the 1998–99 English Premier League season, Derby County finished in 11th position of 20 teams after 38 games. If all the games had ended at halftime Derby would have been the champions! From minute 0 to 60 Derby conceded 24 goals, but from minute 61 to 90 they conceded 25 goals. Derby was a good defensive team when fresh but a poor one when fatigued.

Defining Moments

A soccer game is rhythmic in flow, each team having periods of giving and taking pressure, punctuated with sudden moments that can define the outcome of the game. Players must learn to anticipate these moments when possible and be totally focused and prepared to meet the challenge.

Each week at Derby County the coaches present to the players a short video highlighting the defining moments of the previous game. From experience we have learned that such moments, either for or against us, are often

- the opening minutes of the game, especially away from home,
- the first corner,
- free kicks in dangerous positions,
- reaction after a goal is scored,
- recovering focus after breaks in the game,
- responding to a man being sent off, or
- chasing or closing down the game in the final few minutes.

Coaching for Concentration

Knowing where and when to pay attention, what information to select, and what information to discard in a complex and fast-moving soccer game is a mental skill that coaches must teach players. For it to become a habit that protects the player under pressure, the coach must repeat the lesson at every practice and after every game.

So when working with players the coach must

- ensure physical fitness to counteract fatigue-destroying concentration;
- treat players as individuals and learn their particular concentration styles;
- reinforce concentration on process, not outcome;
- make practice and teaching relevant to game preparation;
- give each player clear instructions on concentration priorities for his or her specific role, job in the team's organization, and job at set pieces (e.g., corners);
- identify concentration lapses with each player (video feedback is useful and gives clear information);
- give the players a game plan that reduces potential distractions and helps them structure their concentration priorities; and
- learn how to regulate arousal levels.

The coach also has an opportunity to improve players' concentration by managing the game environment. The coach can accomplish this by

- arranging a smooth organization to reduce potential for stress on the players,
- developing routines that enhance the players' concentration,
- preventing external distractions from disrupting the process,
- creating an ambience in the dressing room with music or video that diverts the players from internal distractions such as negative thinking and anxiety,
- not worrying if some players want to be alone, and
- not interfering too much.

Summary

Players' attitudes, and therefore performances, are based on their levels of confidence, composure, and concentration. Concentration is a skill players can learn. Through practice, players can develop it into a habit that minimizes lapses in focus, often making the difference in big games. Players should learn how, when, and where in a game to switch on to total focus and intensity and switch off to relaxed, but alert, attention.

Concentration is a skill acquired by appropriate training and repetition. Players can build their ability to concentrate by learning to direct their thoughts and energies to the priority needs of their jobs and by learning to avoid distractions. The coach can help by reinforcing good concentration, punishing damaging lapses, and minimizing potential distractions on game day.

chapter

5

Visualization

Image Becomes Reality

© Bongarts/SportsChrome-USA

Coaches paint pictures—the simpler the better.

Ron Greenwood, England team manager

On the way to winning the 1996 European championships in England, Germany had to play England at the home of English soccer, Wembley Stadium. The coach, knowing that some of his players had never played there before, arranged for the whole squad, players and staff, to take the public tour of the stadium the day before the match. As the loudspeakers dramatically conveyed the English national anthem, the roars of the English fans, and so on, each German player familiarized himself with the environment and began to visualize how he would cope with the potential stress.

A young and talented international player once explained to me that he had trouble sleeping the two nights before a major game because he could not stop playing the game in his mind. He was relieved when I told him I had heard the Olympic decathlon champion, Dan O'Brien, say the same thing. Such visualization is characteristic of many great performers. They have found that running the possibilities of the game through the inner tape in their mind helps their preparation, especially their readiness to cope with potential stressors. They all, of course, see themselves winning and have discovered that what you see is usually what you get.

The most powerful weapon a soccer player has is the mind. Great players are those who demonstrate total control of mind as well as body.

The power of belief as a precursor to success is well documented. I advise players to read the biographies and autobiographies of the great players who have gone before them. This book has constantly reinforced the importance of programming the player's software and building high levels of confidence, concentration, and composure. Coaches can do much of this for the player, but we now move to a mental skill that players can program for themselves, using visualization to develop a powerful and positive inner tape that will effectively control physical response in times of challenge.

Elmer and Alyce Green (1977) beautifully described this process:

> As we begin to realize that we are not totally the victim of genetics, conditioning, and accidents, changes begin to happen in our lives, nature begins to respond to us in a new way, and the things we visualize, even though unlikely, begin to happen with increasing frequency—our bodies tend to do what they are told to do, if we know how to tell them.

To be successful in challenging situations, soccer players need to build strong self-portraits—views of themselves as good players who can cope with whatever comes along. Visualization, using all the senses to re-create or create an experience in the mind, is a process that can train the inner tape of the mind to build that self-portrait. By using vivid imagery, players can re-create the game and all its demands in the mind and develop a mental blueprint that prepares both their confidence and their strategies for coping.

The Process of Visualization

This mental skill requires the player to imagine himself or herself playing soccer—seeing, hearing, feeling, and possibly even smelling the action. To avoid mental clutter and possible disruptions, the player should combine visualization with a state of deep relaxation. The player can then focus sharply on the imagined action, and as Lynch (1986) explains

> the images become so alive that your central nervous system fails to distinguish between a real or imagined event; your body responds to each in the same way. Thus, an athlete who pictures each move of an event correctly in advance will have a greater chance of repeating those moves, having in a sense "practiced" them before the actual event.
>
> Think of visualization as a dress rehearsal. It is a form of practice that makes you familiar with the task.

The player should strive to re-create the sight, physical sensation, sound, and smell of the soccer scene to achieve a more realistic simulation and greater benefit. Now the player will see himself or herself in the scene, choosing the correct course of action, carrying it through with excellent effect, and even hearing the approval of the crowd and positive comment from the coach. The key to visualization is that a positive image of this particular situation now exists in the player's memory. The player can then access it when a similar situation occurs in a match. At the least, by having something to draw on, the player will not be caught completely off guard.

Clearly, the more a player practices visualization, the more accurate the images will become. The memory trace will become stronger, the image more accessible, and the emotional support more powerful, boosting both motivation and confidence. Figure 5.1 outlines the general process of visualization, and table 5.1 gives a clear example of how the player might structure the imaging process.

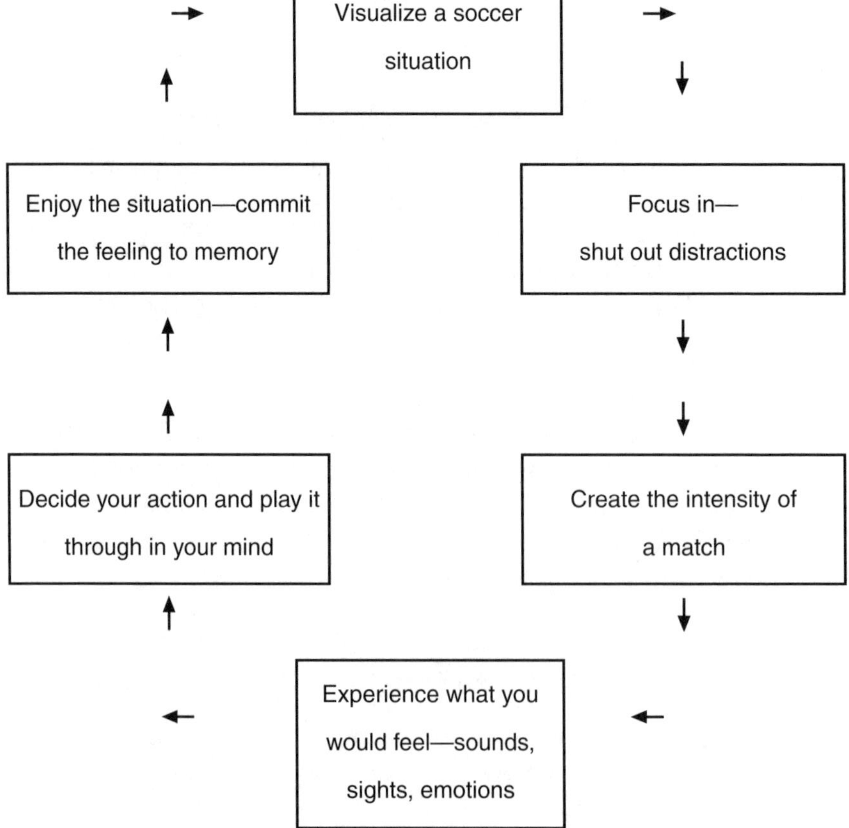

Figure 5.1 The process of visualization.

TABLE 5.1 USING IMAGINATION TO OUR ADVANTAGE

Use this as a guide to creating your own tape with your voice leading you through a structured thought pattern

CONCENTRATE ON VISUALIZING THE SCENE, THE NOISE, THE EMOTIONS, AND SO ON.
1. Get comfortable and close your eyes.
2. Feel good, confident, and proud.
3. Imagine you are in a movie theatre with a big screen while sitting in a comfortable chair.
"You are the star." "You feel good, alive, healthy." "You know it's great to play soccer." "Today is your day." "You feel like a champion." "You are moving well." "Today is your day." "Congratulate yourself." "Feel proud." "You know if a mistake happens, you will talk yourself back to recovery." "Today is your day." "You are tired but satisfied." "You thank your body and mind." "You know you can re-create this feeling anytime you want."

A script from Joel Fish, sports psychologist, presented at a conference of the National Soccer Coaches Association of America, Philadelphia, 1996.

The Benefits of Visualization

Players and coaches who use visualization believe it helps them to

- reinforce self-belief and see themselves as winners,
- learn self-control and develop coping strategies,
- practice mentally what they experience in the game,
- learn to focus and shut out distractions,
- improve relaxation, and
- link mind and body to produce the appropriate energy state.

To maximize benefits, players should observe the following approach:

- Relax—a calm state of mind is essential.
- Use all the senses—the stronger the imagery, the greater the chance of success.
- Visualize in the positive, always seeing or feeling yourself playing well.
- Focus on the process, not going directly to the desired outcome (a snapshot) but imagining the whole process leading up to the performance (a movie).
- Be specific by seeing all the details clearly, leaving nothing out.
- Show belief by being committed to visualization and believing that what you see is what you get.
- Be patient—it will be a while before you see benefits, but short, consistent sessions will lead you there.

Using Visualization to Improve Performance

Although visualization can be used for any performance issue the player or coach would like to rescript, the process has been applied to good effect in specific instances.

Skill Learning and Practice

It has often been demonstrated that the best kind of learning is a combination of visualization, mentally rehearsing the movement and thus programming the software, and physical practice, programming the hardware. David Gilbourne (1999) advocates that players develop imagery scripts in which they visualize in detail the stimulus-response procedure of a particular skill on the pitch (see table 5.2). In this written account of the visualization practice, the player would be required to pay great attention to all the details involved in the image:

> For example, a typical script may include references to situational factors such as other players, the ball, the feel of studs in the ground, the noise of the crowd, the sense of movement, changes in the muscular tension as a player recalls accelerating,

TABLE 5.2 AN IMAGERY SCRIPT FOR TECHNICAL DEVELOPMENT

Technique: Crossing the ball at pace and hitting to the far post

STIMULUS PROPOSITIONS:
1. I see the defender trying to force me in-field.
2. I hear the center forward shouting, "Take him on."
3. I see the ball at my feet and my knee over the ball.
RESPONSE PROPOSITIONS:
4. I feel my shoulder dip as I fake an inside move. At the same time my left foot pushes the ball forward.
5. I drive hard with my right leg, feel the ground under my boot, feel my arms drive (as I accelerate after the ball).
6. I think, "Cross with pace."
STIMULUS PROPOSITIONS:
7. I glance into the penalty area and see Steve peeling away from the far post.
8. I switch focus onto the ball.
RESPONSE PROPOSITIONS:
9. I think, "I have to lift the ball over the defender."
10. I adjust my stride and feel my legs hit the right tempo and rhythm.
11. I feel my body lean away and whip my left foot around the ball.
12. I feel my body overbalance as I watch the ball arc into the penalty box.
Source: Gilbourne, D. 1999. Insight—The Football Coaches Association Journal. Issue 3, Volume 2.

twisting, jumping, or landing, an awareness of accompanying emotions and so on.

Understanding Tactics and Strategy

To perform well, a player must understand the tactical shape of the team and his or her role within it. When a team must change tactics quickly and significantly—as often happens with national teams playing tournament soccer—the only preparation available may be to take the whole team through a visualization process that uses the form, "If this happens . . . then we will . . ."

Warming Up Mentally

Players have many different ways of warming up mentally for a game. Most include some form of visualization—rehearsing the game in their minds. Players often sit quietly and mentally rehearse the concentration they need for their first involvement in the game—first touch, first tackle, first header, and so on. I often tell strikers that their first touch may be the best opportunity to score in the whole 90 minutes—so be ready! Players can also try to capture on a reminder card the essence of their game in 8 or 10 words or short phrases and then read it just before the game.

Rehearsing Performance Routines

Although players often play on automatic, letting their habits take over, in situations such as penalties, corners, and free kicks, players have time to think and can therefore rehearse their actions. An increasingly important aspect of soccer is the penalty shootout. Although it is impossible to reproduce the shootout exactly on the practice field, with visualization we can prepare the players' minds for the surge of emotion and help them create disciplined performance routines that they can hold on to. Then on that long walk from the center circle, they can be rehearsing an approved routine that not only helps them avoid distractions but also boosts confidence at a vital time.

Managing Stress

All players feel stress, but successful players learn to cope with it. Some even learn to thrive on it. With players who are susceptible to stress, I use visualization as a way of rescripting emotional expectations. When such a player visualizes a challenging game, he or she normally sees moments of potential stress and negatively programs the inner tape. A coach, sports psychologist, or fellow player can change this picture by reminding the player of his or her ability, experience, past success, strength of the team, and so on.

I often ask a player, "What's the worst thing that can happen—and can you live with it?" The best visualization involves feelings, using the following imagery pattern:

- What if this (potential source of stress) happens?
- How will I feel?

- Then I will . . .
- And therefore I will regain control.

So, for example, a player receives a yellow card, feels angry and guilty, but remembers to stay out of further trouble for the sake of the team and therefore regains control.

Relaxation techniques such as meditation and yoga can aid this entire process.

Building Confidence

Clearly, the more a player sees himself or herself as a winner, the more the player is likely to perform that way. Teams must find ways of reminding players how good they can be (not how poor) if they want them to have the inner strength to face competitive challenge. The message must be strong enough that eventually the image becomes reality. At Derby County I helped turn around a somewhat critical culture to one based more on positive reinforcement. Players receive many more positive strokes, and we supported this with highlight videos that featured all the players doing things well. Players with strong self-esteem are far more likely to receive criticism of performance without damage. Their inner tape will still show them as winners.

Recovering From Injury

A sudden injury—and the resultant withdrawal from the excitement and involvement of team participation—can often damage a player psychologically as much as it does physically. As always, the player has a choice about how to regard the injury:

- The player may take a negative view by thinking, "This is awful."
- The player might be more positive and say, "Unfortunately, this has happened—how soon will I be back playing, and what do I have to do?"

The player's support group—coaches, medical team, other players, family—has the job of encouraging the player to visualize the injury and rehabilitation in strong, positive ways. Although the player cannot practice physically during rehabilitation, visualization promotes some maintenance of skills during recovery. Many physiotherapists believe this helps speed the healing process.

Managing Energy

The mind and the body are so strongly linked that when a player visualizes an action the body begins to prepare a response. If the player learns to visualize positively, the body will prepare for action in a positive manner with increased energy. Players who visualize negatively will experience the reverse.

Coaches who are aware of this effect will be careful to present players with messages and images about the next game that evoke the required visualization and therefore induce the correct energy state. Figure 5.2 shows that the most successful players, who

	Player images →	Emotional state →	Energy state →	Performance state
A	– The winner – The best – In control	– Excitement – Happiness	– High – Positive	– Activated – Committed – Confident
B	– Unhurried – Easy going – Relaxed	– Contented – Calm	– Low – Positive	– Passive – Unmotivated – Vulnerable
C	– Irate – Frustrated – Revengeful	– Anger – Excitement	– High – Negative	– Destructive – Damaging – Out of control
D	– Depressed – Powerless – Tired	– Fear – Sadness	– Low – Negative	– Passive – Unwilling – Victim

Figure 5.2 The effect of visualization on a player's energy and performance.

visualize positively, will be in a state of high positive energy. This describes exactly the point of relaxed readiness that we try to produce in our England players just before game time.

Players complacent or not fully aroused will find themselves in a state of low positive energy—a relaxing place but not where we want to be for winning. Without proper mental preparation, a team may find itself there after taking a lead, thinking to themselves, "The pressure is off so relax."

Players who don't care or feel overwhelmed will produce low negative energy. Coaches hired to turn things around often find their new teams in this state. Changing the way the players visualize themselves and their situation is an immediate priority.

Finally, the most dangerous state of mind is high negative. Players find themselves in uncontrolled passion, negatively burning up energy. Where a team or player is not mentally disciplined, an adverse incident in a game or even pregame can throw them completely out of control and reduce the chances of winning. Coaches often use anger to inject energy into a team, but they must ensure that the player or team is mature enough mentally to channel it in a positive direction.

The Chris Powell Story

Chris, a talented and mature fullback at Derby, was asked to extend his normal defensive role to that of a wingback, therefore having an attacking assignment as well as defending responsibilities. Chris was clearly failing to make this change when he came to see me. Through discussion with Chris, consultation with the coaches, and video analysis of Chris in action, it became clear that he was physically and technically capable of being an outstanding wingback. Equally clear was that he couldn't commit mentally or emotionally to the position.

I encouraged Chris to use the process of visualization to imagine scenes from games in which he would be playing as a wingback. From this we began to identify (a) an accurate job description that encompassed all physical, technical, and tactical demands, and (b) the thoughts and feelings Chris associated with each of these demands.

(continued)

We were able to establish that the problem was one of confidence and assertiveness. For Chris, defending was a science that allowed him to exert maximum control, whereas attacking was a gamble with increasing risk. Therefore, his confidence and assertiveness drained away as he crossed the halfway line to join the attack.

So we began a process of helping Chris mentally simulate—by private visualization, discussion, and video review—the movements, thoughts, and feelings linked with positive attacking from wingback. We always emphasized that Chris should develop an image of a successful attacking play and try to involve all the senses that accompanied the action. We monitored progress through weekly analysis and observation of the contributions Chris made in the attacking half of the field. The coaching staff and I offered great praise and reinforcement for progress.

Slowly we removed the mental and emotional barriers in his mind and reinforced his belief. Chris began to show much greater confidence and assertiveness when attacking. Instead of hiding, he began to demand the ball. Chris overcame the problem, scoring two goals in the Premier League and being elected club Player of the Year, demonstrating that players can mentally shift gears to undertake new responsibilities on the pitch. Visualization is one of the tools at their disposal. Clear the mind, and the feet will follow.

Summary

Visualization is a mental tool that some players and teams find helpful in preparing their minds to meet the challenge of the game. A clear link has been established between positive thinking and the likelihood of positive action, so players are encouraged to spend time visualizing themselves performing with excellence. What you see is often what you get.

Visualization is recommended for building confidence, developing strategies to cope with stress, understanding tactics and strategy, and assisting recovery from injury. Of great importance is the link between visualization—how we see ourselves—and our emotional state, our energy state, and therefore our potential for performance. As we exercise the mind it grows stronger. The more the player pictures success, the more energy he or she creates to achieve it.

chapter

6

Mental Toughness

Building a Winning Attitude

© Action Images

Mental toughness is many things and rather difficult to explain. Its qualities are sacrifice and self-denial. Also most importantly, it is combined with a perfectly disciplined will that refuses to give in. It's a state of mind—you could call it character in action.

Vincent T. Lombardi

After a 1-1 draw at home, Manchester United traveled to Italy to play Juventus in the second leg of the 1999 European club championships semifinal. The television commentator reminded us that Juventus had not lost a European championship match at home for 14 years, and that it had been 31 years since United had last won the European championship. In a tense and intimidating atmosphere, Juventus scored two goals in the first 12 minutes. Heads went down all over England—except among the 11 players in red. They showed true mental toughness and remained positive in the face of adversity in coming back to win the game 3-2!

In the week following I was invited to spend a day with United. I decided I would try to discover the basis of such mental toughness. What immediately struck me was the tremendous internal competition within the squad. Players felt free to challenge each other to be better, and they dealt harshly with lack of quality.

A series of hurdles appeared to be in place for each player, which ensured that only the mentally toughest would survive:

Hurdle 1: United recruits only the best—it's tough to get there.

Hurdle 2: From 47 professionals only 16 make the first-team squad.

Hurdle 3: The standard at practice is so high and so competitive that any weakness in technique or attitude is exposed constantly and heavily criticized by fellow players.

Hurdle 4: Only 11 players make the team, and there is a lot of choice.

Hurdle 5: Sixty-seven thousand spectators and a worldwide television audience expect United to win. One bad day and a player can be out of the team for some time.

Hurdle 6: The possibility of injury is always present, so players must constantly worry about having to start over to win back a place on the team.

After that day I was no longer surprised at the way the team maintained confidence, self-control, and concentration after going two goals down in Italy. The ability to cope with such pressure is an everyday survival skill of these players.

Of course, all human activities are challenging, but being successful at soccer—an activity that publicly labels players as winners or losers—requires great mental and emotional strength alongside physical and technical excellence. A youth soccer team that easily wins all its games will be highly praised, but the players will be mentally and emotionally unprepared when they move up a level and start to lose games. As Ravizza and Hanson (1995) so beautifully expressed it, "Failure is part of the Dance." The mentally tough player must be able to live with insecurity, treat setbacks as part of the price to be paid, and withstand what may seem like constant criticism.

In the 1998–99 Premier League season, Derby County played 38 games, won 13, drew 13, and lost 12. One of the factors that characterized the team's mental toughness was the ability to handle the dips—the periods of the season when everything seemed to be going wrong. Each week we programmed the software as well as the hardware as we analyzed defeats, placed them in the perspective of the season, let them go, and then refocused on a positive approach that underlined the benefits of staying resolute in the face of adversity.

So important is this ability to recover from setbacks that Goldberg (1998) concludes, "The feelings of failure are in reality the doorway to ultimate success . . . of all the physical and mental qualities a player may possess, mental toughness is the most important."

Mental Toughness Is a Winning Attitude

Throughout this book are numerous examples reinforcing the principle that performance follows attitude. So the starting point for a player or team wishing to become mentally tougher has to be creating a positive and winning attitude. Mental toughness is the ability to impose physically what a player is committed to mentally. If that commitment wavers because of a setback then clearly performance will be a step closer to failure.

Players and coaches must create a training and competition culture that constantly shapes the state of mind in a positive and confident way. Mental toughness is a state of mind that players can develop by applying these principles:

- Think like a winner. Show high self-belief and expect to win: "Positive visions lead to positive realities—they always have and they always will." (Orlick 1986)
- Turn negatives into positives. Treat setbacks as an inevitable part of the challenge and learn from them to become a more complete player.
- Deal with the unexpected. Regard demanding, changing conditions as the ultimate challenge, enjoy being tested, and believe that "tough times don't last, tough people do."

We have already established in this book that a positive state of mind leads to positive emotions and the high positive energy needed for successful performance. Table 6.1 illustrates the same process, albeit a little simplistically, with an example of how two players—one mentally tough, the other not—might react to a missed chance of scoring.

Four Steps to Mental Toughness

The ideal performance state and the mental toughness we seek are characterized by a clear sense of purpose and direction, a high

TABLE 6.1 MENTALLY TOUGH VS. MENTALLY WEAK

Comparison of a mentally tough player with a mentally weak player after missing a good chance to score

	MENTALLY TOUGH	MENTALLY WEAK
Attitude change	Thinks, "I'll get the next one," remains positive, and does not lose self-belief	Thinks, "I'll never score now," becomes instantly negative, and loses all self-belief
Emotional response	Remains enthusiastic, stimulated, and vigorous	Becomes irritated and discouraged, loses hope, and blames others
Resultant energy state	Remains positive in direction and high in intensity	Becomes negative in direction and low in intensity
Effect on performance	More likely to recover well and score with a later chance	Becomes increasingly passive, hides, and is more concerned with not missing again than working for another chance to score

degree of resilience, emotional calmness, and the fuel of high positive energy. The following steps, then, should become essential elements of players' training and competition routines.

Step One: Develop Strong Self-Identity

Our performance is often the result of our expectations, so unless we think and feel like winners we are unlikely to perform like winners. Players should check themselves for the following practices, which can help develop a winning state of mind:

- Remember you are already a winner—recall all your previous successes.
- Always look good—reflect the image of a winner.
- Control your thoughts and allow only positive self-talk.
- Be your own cheerleader—reward yourself at every sign of progress.
- Become more assertive in imposing yourself on the situation.
- Take responsibility for your actions—excuses are the first signs of weakness.
- Be persistent—do not accept failure too easily.
- Be consistent to make confidence a habit—don't fluctuate between confidence and fear.
- Keep learning—the battle is never won.
- Copy role models to help develop positive and winning behaviors.

When coach Tony Pickard helped convert tennis star Stefan Edberg from an anxious loser to an assertive winner, he used a combination of positive self-talk and confident body language. "Fix the body language and the mind stands tall."

Step Two: Become and Stay Motivated

The most important question a player must answer is why he or she commits to the challenge, accepts the criticism, and deals with possible failure. It takes courage to cross the white line at the start of a match. A player can reach that level of arousal only by being fully motivated.

Commitment to play is a choice, and nothing can affect performance as dramatically as a sudden loss of motivation. Without

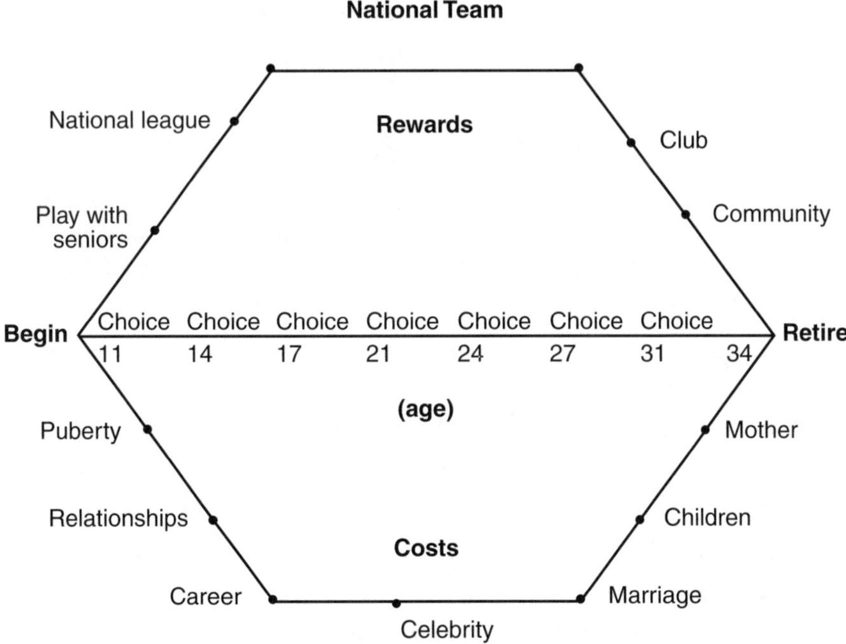

Figure 6.1 Rewards vs. costs at various stages of a female player's career.

motivation, without the drive to achieve, the player cannot develop the mental toughness to survive the challenge of soccer. Problems become barriers, not challenges.

After working with the England national women's team, I became more aware of how much more difficult the choice of playing soccer can be for women players. Figure 6.1 shows that throughout a woman's soccer career, in the important life years of 14 to 34 years of age, she will continually face the dilemma of choosing between the potential rewards of soccer and social and family life.

The sources of motivation are both intrinsic and extrinsic. A mentally tough competitor will be self-motivated and self-directed. This player is involved because he or she wants to be.

Figure 6.2 identifies how the player's motivation must move through certain stages or challenges before becoming an intrinsic element of mental toughness. In the early stages, family and friends motivate players. Players then move on to the more critical influence of the coach. Of course, many players do not survive

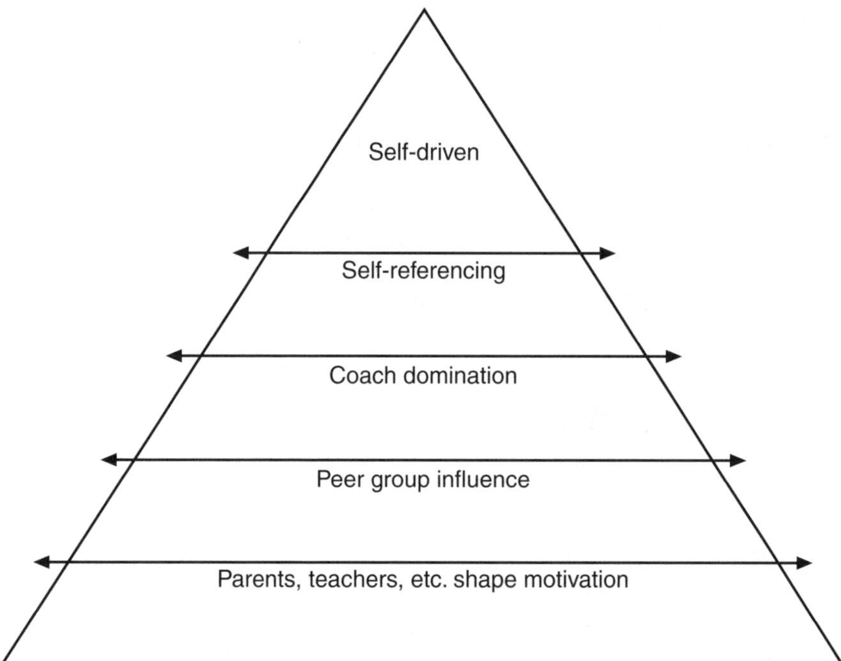

Figure 6.2 The route to self-motivation and mental toughness.

these stages and drop out because they lack either physical ability or mental strength.

The final stage, when motivation switches from extrinsic to intrinsic, is when mental toughness becomes critical. The player is now driven by comparisons with players he or she admires and a desire to perform to potential. Rather than relying on the views of others, the player now checks his or her performance against personal standards. Although not isolated from external influences, the player now controls his or her state of mind and is much tougher mentally.

It helps, of course, if the player's social support group is positive and supportive in the journey to excellence. Although male players benefit from both intrinsic and extrinsic sources of motivation, women soccer players may not receive complete social support at certain stages in their development. They must rely on their intrinsic drive to play, which may be why I found them such mentally tough individuals.

Step Three: Establish a Work Ethic

For a player to feel positive and confident about the challenge of a tough match, he or she must feel physically capable of meeting the expected demands. Any questions about fitness, strength, and energy potential will begin to sow the seeds of doubt and anxiety, undermining performance before the player steps on the pitch. This may be a significant issue for

- the young player in his or her debut,
- the older player near the end of a career,
- the player returning from injury,
- players faced with too many matches and insufficient recovery,
- the player with poor diet and nutrition,
- the player with a damaging lifestyle,
- the player playing out of position, and
- the player who has been asked to play too long or too often and has simply burned out.

Motivation and confidence are inextricably linked with the willingness and capacity to work hard to ensure the best chance of success. When coaches and players work hard to prepare for a match, they build a belief that they have paid the price for victory. By committing to the effort, they become not only physically tougher but also mentally tougher. As Coach Vince Lombardi (Kramer 1970) says, "The harder we prepare, the harder it is to surrender."

Players, especially younger players, should read the autobiographies of former great players, in soccer and in other sports. They will find again and again the message of the importance of having a work ethic. Julius Erving, the legendary Dr. J of basketball, says that it took him a whole career to be an overnight success. Nick Price, the golfer, emphasizes that it took him the whole of the 1980s to become an accomplished player in the 1990s.

Mentally tough players are the product of not only hard work but also smart work. They know when to work hard and when to recover. Within their training and lifestyle they will incorporate good diet and nutrition, sufficient sleep, relaxation, and massage. Their self-discipline will always triumph over temptation—alcohol, drugs, and tobacco will not disrupt or harm their development.

Chapter 1 emphasizes that mental development can take pl alongside physical development, so the smart player and coac will create a training program that allows for both. Figure 1.2 in that chapter shows that intense practice should be based on whole-player excellence. Thus, the drills force players to work at high intensity while remaining mentally focused and making good decisions. When the going gets tough, the mentally tough player gets going!

Step Four: Develop Self-Control

Being mentally tough means being positive in the face of adversity, especially when an occurrence in the match produces an emotional surge that the player struggles to control. Loehr and McLaughlin (1990) identify the four responses the player may make when problems lead to emotional change:

1. The player may tank, withdrawing energy and commitment.
2. The player may become angry, allowing energy to turn negative.
3. The player may choke, becoming nervous and afraid.
4. The player may respond to the challenge by investing additional positive energy to deal with the problem, the mentally tough way.

Mentally tough players see problems and setbacks as part of the territory if they wish to compete in soccer. When setbacks occur, they have the self-belief to view them as challenges to overcome. The player cannot choose what happens, but he or she can choose how to respond.

Dealing with criticism, mistakes, and victory or defeat is essential to a player's development. Therefore, much of my work with Derby County and England is preparing the players for likely scenarios through discussion and videos and then reviewing the potential actions. The players and I would examine examples of tanking, loss of temper, and choking before agreeing that exercising the self-control to meet the challenge is the best answer. The real tough guy is not the one who lashes out and loses control but the one who keeps control and walks away—the opposite of the common belief!

Slump

pecially important when a player or team goes is often the time I choose to undertake a tional health check, reminding players why they must continue to face up to the challenge.

At the end of the 1998-99 season Derby County had achieved two of its three agreed-on objectives, but the team experienced a losing run and faced an uphill struggle in the final eight games of the season. To achieve the third goal, a place in the top six, the boys needed some prompting from me to remind them why they should stay committed. I put several thoughts before them:

- Courage—the greatest bravery in soccer is wanting the ball when your team is not doing well. Are you making things happen on the pitch?
- Love—the best motivation is love of playing, so don't let results overcome your enjoyment of this great game. Ask yourselves what you would be doing if you weren't a soccer professional.
- Excellence is a habit—great performance is based on good habits, and habits are created by repetition. Good players know they can't switch their attitude and performance on and off.
- Staying in the game—we can control only what we do, we cannot control our opponents, and we cannot predict their state of mind. We must stay competitive as long as possible. Our opponents may suddenly collapse and present us with the chance to achieve.
- Who we are—how we face the dips in form and how we stay competitive and strong together sends a message to our opponents. We win their respect, which gives us an advantage when we meet them again. Dealing with a slump defines players as people, as more than just players.
- Keep learning—Arrigo Saaci, the great Italian coach, once said, "The greatest quality of the greatest players is humility." By that he meant that they never stop learning. Every day, every practice, every match, is an opportunity for these players to learn something new or groove old habits even more

efficiently. These players always have that 1 or 2 percent advantage over other players.

- Achieving targets—at the start of the season each player sets positive but realistic goals for themselves. Achieving them will be a source of great satisfaction and renewed motivation.

By programming the Derby players' software in this way, we raised motivation and mental toughness and fought our way out of our slump.

Coaching for Mental Toughness

The attitude and behavior of the coach strongly influences the performance of the players. Coaches cannot expect to have a mentally tough team unless they plan a program that emphasizes and reinforces positive winning attitudes.

The Coach As a Role Model

The coach is an important and influential authority figure in players' lives. The body language, attitude, and expressions of the coach can shape, reinforce, or damage the players' self-esteem and confidence. This is especially true for younger players in a society with increasing numbers of one-parent families.

If mental toughness is about meeting challenges with positive self-control, then the starting point, both in practice and competition, must be the coach. Never is the coach more tested than after a defeat. As Coach Parcells (1995) explains, "A coach lives in a black and white world—you win or you lose—and the black side stays with you longer."

The aftermath of defeat is a tough moment for a coach. He or she can choose to yell or sell, but the coach who wants a mentally tough team must demonstrate a controlled way to deal with emotional setbacks despite personal feelings. The coach will find that a disciplined postmatch routine is helpful in ensuring that he or she does not get either too high or too low.

Creating the Mind-Set

Jim Thompson (1995) neatly describes the impact of the coach on the team's mind-set and performance: (a) achievement needs energy, (b) energy comes from emotions, (c) emotions are released by ideas, and (d) ideas come from coaches.

So the successful coach will use ideas, stories, metaphors, videos, and so on to shape the collective mind-set of the team and prepare them to be mentally tough in performance. If the coach shows an unwavering belief in the team's ability to achieve despite the obstacles, then the team has a framework for building the same mind-set and will become increasingly motivated.

Learning Through Failure

Handling mistakes and failure is another important area of responsibility for the coach. The coach's reaction to failure is key to the players' motivation and desire to work hard to correct mistakes. The coach has two choices:

- Use failure as an opportunity to give the players feedback on how to improve. Persuade them to recommit themselves to the effort with renewed motivation.
- Use failure as evidence of the players' inadequacy and proof that they cannot meet expectations. This emotional overreaction will demotivate the players.

Goldberg (1998) explains why coaches must avoid the second option: "Your emotional reaction to failure can often blind your perspective and interfere with your ability to bounce back."

Preparing Players Emotionally

If mental toughness is a state of mind, then coaches must integrate its development into every aspect of preparing players. Therefore, practice must

- be seen as relevant and purposeful,
- engage the players' attention so they buy into the hard work,
- simulate game conditions so opportunities are available to create scenarios that build mental toughness, and
- create balance and harmony—including work, recovery, and an element of fun to relieve pressure—so players begin to understand energy management.

By controlling the mood of the players at training, often under exacting conditions, the coach is preparing the players emotionally for competition. When the pressure comes, the players then have a solution bank of responses and are not surprised and caught off-balance.

Solutions When a Team Chokes

Competence in practice but failure in competition became an important issue at Derby County after the team was promoted from Division 1 to the Premier League. In the first season the team felt comfortable in the role of newcomer and outsider because any win was greeted ecstatically and defeats were understood. After a successful first season, however, expectations grew, and Derby was under pressure to win. Favorites have no comfort zone. After a run of three results in which Derby choked and lost after being in the lead, the manager, Jim Smith, asked my opinion. It was clear that the team started the game in a confident, relaxed state. But after taking a lead, and therefore being expected to win, the team began to worry about the outcome (thinking in the future), lost focus and intensity (by not thinking in the present), and performed poorly. The signs indicated the problem.

- Increased anxiety—seeing the situation as stressful
- Loss of focus—increase in unforced errors
- Becoming passive or trying too hard—losing the flow
- Negative self-talk—low expectation of success
- Feelings of little self-control—players asking, "What can I do?"
- Becoming a 60-minute team, not a 90-minute team

The solutions that the coaches, players, and I agreed on and worked toward were the following:

- Becoming aware that our emotional state might change.
- Reading the signals that would tell us when the change might occur (after a goal, for example).
- Players, especially seniors, taking responsibility and not looking for excuses.
- Becoming more assertive when we lead. After a score we

take the view that we should score again! England under-21 has a rule that we will never allow our opponents more than three passes from the re-start after we have scored. This tactic ensures an assertive and focused attitude.

- Concentrating on the present—not allowing future thoughts.
- Never allowing ourselves to become passive.
- Increasing communication by all.
- Changing beliefs, believing that we can win every game.

Two seasons later, Derby is firmly based in the Premier League, can handle high expectations, rarely chokes, and is much tougher mentally in facing challenges.

Self-Referencing

One way that players become mentally tough is by accepting responsibility for their thoughts, feelings, and actions and rejecting all possible excuses. Coaches can help by questioning and listening—not always telling players what they did wrong but encouraging them to talk about what they could have done better.

Perhaps the most complete basketball player ever, Michael Jordan (1994) was strong on this aspect of mental toughness:

> Players always want to blame someone else or some circumstance out of their control for their problems. You find a way not to accept the blame. The better players learn to say, "I played bad, but tomorrow I'll play better." A lot of younger players are afraid to admit they have bad nights, but everybody has bad nights, and it's how you rebound from these bad nights that dictates what kind of player you are going to be!

The coach can play a part in this by always encouraging the player to self-reference. Instead of giving the player a definition of the situation, the coach can ask the player to explain his or her actions—"How do you feel you played?" or "Why do you feel you behaved that way?" In this way the player must think through and account for his or her actions—a vital part of the learning process. The coach might borrow a thought from Rudyard Kipling for the notice board: "We have 40 million reasons, but not a single excuse."

Summary

To excel at a challenging activity like soccer and have the ability to recover from the inevitable setbacks along the way, players and coaches must possess a high degree of mental toughness, defined as the ability to impose physically what is committed to mentally. It is clearly the result of developing a winning attitude.

This state of mind consists of a strong self-identity, high intrinsic motivation, a good work ethic, and excellent self-control in pressure situations. As a role model for the players, the coach must demonstrate mental toughness in preparing for games, coping with the emotional nature of the contest, and dealing with mistakes and failure.

Mental toughness starts with the personality and attitudes of the individual player, but it is enhanced by a team culture that consistently reinforces the value of being positive in the face of adversity.

chapter

7

Competitiveness

Mental Preparation and Power for Matches

© Action Images

Now, if you're going to win any battle, you have to do one thing. You have to make the mind run the body. Never let the body tell the mind what to do.

General George S. Patton Jr.

Ten minutes before young Lee Morris made his debut at home for Derby County, he vomited down the front of his match shirt. None of the players in the dressing room were particularly concerned, and the trainer helped Lee clean himself up. All the players in the room were anxious, but experience had taught them to cope in different ways.

I moved over to Lee, looked him in the eyes, and quietly said, "When you cross that white line all you are going to find is a large piece of grass, 22 players, one ball, and one referee—no different than you have dealt with since you started playing at eight years of age. Trust your habits and enjoy yourself."

Lee found his inner strength and within minutes had the crowd on its feet with a wonderful run on goal. As I thought would happen, his instinctive competitiveness had taken over from his fear. Later I told Lee what Bruce Jenner (1996), the former Olympic decathlon champion, said about converting fear from negative to positive: "Use the fear as something you are running away from."

As this and many other examples in this book show, it is only in the challenge of competition that players discover their true strengths and weaknesses. The more demanding the competition, the more thoroughly each player's physical, technical, mental, and emotional qualities will be tested. Once a player reveals a weakness, opponents will be quick to seize on it.

No player is perfect, but every player should aim to become more complete by assessing his or her personal profile and learning to maximize it. All great players have a unique personal formula for performing well. Each player must find what works for him or her in preparation to play.

The comedian Woody Allen once said that 80 percent of success is just showing up. In sports, the starting point for players is finding the courage to overcome the fears that the challenge of competition produces. "We promise with our hopes, but we perform with our fears." Players have to recognize, internalize, and accept the following fears each time they play:

- They might fail.
- They might succeed and then face more demanding expectations.
- Their weaknesses might be exposed.
- They might be rejected through nonselection or substitution.
- They might sustain a serious injury.
- They might face something they didn't expect and not be able to cope with it.

A question that players must answer is what makes them overcome those fears and commit to soccer.

Achieving Peak Competitiveness

Figure 7.1 illustrates the route that players must take if they wish to reach the highest level of competitive form—the state of flow.

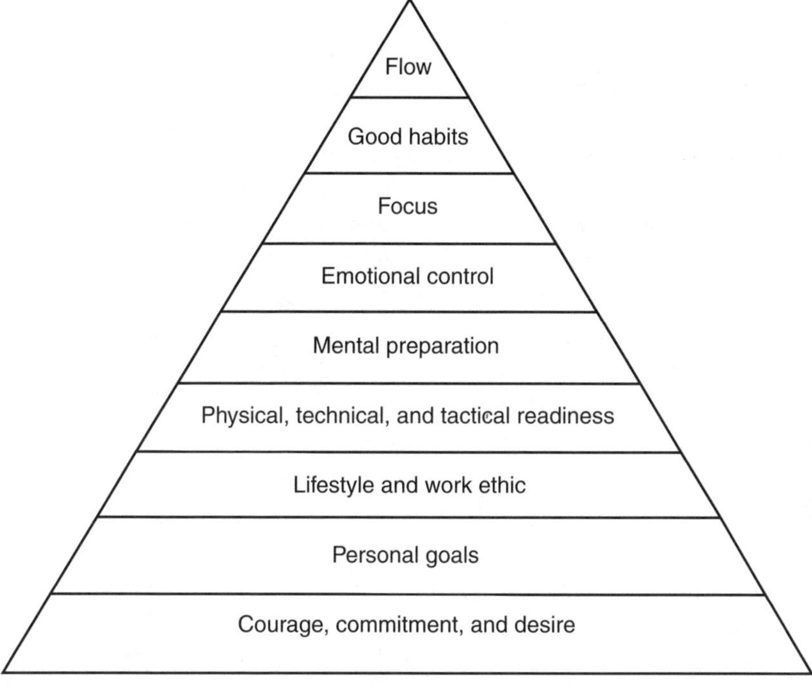

Figure 7.1 The route to the state of flow.

This journey represents a personal game plan for players, who should check their strengths or weaknesses with their coaches at each stage.

Key points for each stage are explained below.

1. Courage, commitment, and desire—the starting point for players who undertake this difficult journey is a dream that inspires and motivates them to face up to the challenge. Unless a player dreams of being the best it is unlikely that he or she will find the motivation to overcome the hurdles along the way.

2. Personal goals—the player lacking direction can waste energy and determination, so each player should spend time establishing personal goals, both long term and short term. I sometimes stop players and ask them why they have to come to practice. They generally respond, "To improve." I then ask, "Improve what?" and so on. This sort of conversation helps players realize that practice is the best opportunity for working on their personal goals and reminds them why they need to make the effort.

3. Lifestyle and work ethic—"You play how you live" is often quoted to young players. The greatest challenge to young well-paid professionals may well be lifestyle issues. Lifestyle usually has its most dramatic effect on work ethic. I once heard Dan O'Brien, the Olympic decathlon champion, respond to the question about how he became the champion. He wrote two numbers on the board—1,500 and 36—and then explained that it took him 1,500 hours of training to prepare for 36 minutes of explosive activity on the track. O'Brien knows that only in the dictionary does success come before work and that living a healthy lifestyle is the only way to manage such a workload.

4. Physical, technical, and tactical readiness—we cannot achieve a state of flow if we are fatigued, if we cannot control the ball, or if we are confused about tactical decisions. Fundamental preparation, often more about perspiration than inspiration, underpins success. To achieve competitive excellence, players must know that they can do their job physically, technically, and tactically.

5. Mental preparation—having made the commitment and worked hard to prepare physically and technically, players must convert the effort into a winning attitude. From good preparation should come a strong sense of self-identity, confidence, and the foundations of mental toughness. Obstacles and setbacks will

inevitably delay progress, so success may well depend on the player's ability to stay mentally positive and resilient.

6. Emotional control—having created the right frame of mind and a competitive attitude, players must establish a personal strategy to maintain it under pressure on the emotional roller coaster of soccer. Physically, the player is well prepared to compete, but games take place in an emotional context. The discipline of emotional control is essential to preventing the mind from getting in the way of the body. Flow is sometimes defined as the absence of emotional static. You cannot flow if you are not in control of your emotions.

7. Focus—players need mental power to bring maximum focus to key moments of the game. Applying intense focus expends a great amount of energy. Mentally tough players understand the need for proper recovery and relaxation—they come to each game with their batteries recharged.

When Dan O'Brien was asked about the most important skill he had learned, he replied that it was the skill of forgetting, or letting go. He emphasized the importance of being able to clear the mind after being involved in one piece of action, especially one with a negative result, in order to be focused, positive, and relaxed for the next.

8. Good habits—the state of flow is often described as a no-think situation in which the body works automatically. Trust is an important ingredient. Players will perform best if they get their minds—and possible doubts and anxieties—out of the way and trust the habits they have programmed into their bodies. I work every week with players who survive important games not on new behavior they suddenly create but on good habits established over many years of work. Train and trust!

Thus the journey to competitiveness and flow calls for a great deal of responsibility on the part of the player. But that's what separates the great players from the rest. Here, too, players can learn much by reading accounts of the great players in all sports, not only soccer. For example, Halberstam's (1999) wonderful analysis of Michael Jordan's career illustrates many aspects of competitiveness and shows how Michael became the most competitive team player in the world—playing in the flow night after night.

Jacob Loses His Competitive Edge

Jacob Laursen, a Danish international and captain of Derby County, was not happy personally or with his form when he came to see me. After some discussion, it became apparent that Jacob's loss of competitive edge was due to a number of problems, personal and soccer, that were clouding his mind and demotivating him:

- Recent separation from his wife and children
- Pressure to return to Denmark
- Uncertainty about his role as captain
- Frustration about not playing in his best position
- Concern about the generally disappointing performance of the team

We agreed immediately to focus on controlling the controllables and to park anything we could not influence on an imaginary shelf. Jacob then agreed to attack his lifestyle issues by seeking expert advice and creating an action plan.

The next stage was for Jacob to deal with his soccer concerns and share them with the only person who could affect them—the manager. Jim Smith, as always, was tremendously supportive. He relieved Jacob of the burden of captaincy and soon found a way to restore him to his strongest position.

Finally, Jacob and I revisited his personal goals for the season. A proud man, Jacob sets high standards, and he agreed that he should not let them slip because his team was performing poorly.

Providing an excellent example of "clearing the mind to clear the feet," Jacob became happier and almost immediately regained his competitive edge.

Being Competitive on Match Day

We can now assume that the player has prepared well and brings good physical and mental skills to his or her performance. The more ingrained these skills are, the greater the probability of success. Now we can concentrate on the approach to match day and building the ideal competitive state.

Mental and Emotional Preparation on Match Day—10 Ways to Build Competitive Power

1. Visualize what the game may be like, see yourself as the star, and focus on a superb performance.
2. Remember that you are a winner—focus on the success that got you here.
3. Allow only positive self-talk; avoid moaners.
4. Use inspirational material that helps you develop your arousal.
5. Minimize potential disruptions and become comfortable with the game location.
6. Practice relaxation.
7. Maintain perspective—it's another day at the office—and control your emotions.
8. Mentally rehearse the important elements of your job.
9. Follow the pregame routine that makes you feel comfortable and prepares you to play.
10. Trust your habits and enjoy the challenge.

Pregame

I always remind players that pregame starts much earlier than their arrival in the dressing room. It is their responsibility to have a clear mind and be well rested after dealing with family and other potential distractions.

Players differ in style and routine of preparation. Areas must be found in the dressing room for the introvert, who will prefer space and privacy, and the extrovert, who can follow a routine while happily interacting with others.

Although styles will vary, each player must have a routine that clears the mind and allows him or her to begin to focus on soccer issues. Table 4.2 (page 60) shows how the England under-18 team prepares for a game.

Each player must build a pregame competitive state by

- thinking and acting in a totally positive manner,
- ignoring any negatives,

- talking themselves up,
- getting control of their emotions,
- building arousal by reminding themselves why the game is important,
- slowly narrowing focus and increasing intensity, and
- reviewing constantly the three most important things they will do to contribute to their team's success.

Players must accomplish all this while being relaxed and enjoying the moment. Of course, experience is a major factor in developing sound pregame coping strategies.

Coaches try various ways to influence the mental state of their players in the dressing room—motivational talks, humor, video, music, wall posters, cue cards, and so on. As a final way of shaping positive attitudes at Derby, we engage in a team huddle on the pitch at the end of the warm-up. Each week I give the captain an appropriate message to feed the team—for example, "We can only win by sticking together."

The Game

As General Norman Schwarzkopf said, "All planning is spoilt by contact with the enemy," and there is nothing like the game for spoiling all that nice pregame preparation. A team may occasionally maintain the pregame state of mind for the whole 90 minutes, but the opponent will usually produce difficult and unsettling moments. The player must now reveal mental toughness by thriving on the pressure.

The bottom line is control—the player must first exert self-control and then exercise control over the opponents and the game situations he or she is involved in. As we have emphasized, in the heat of the game the player relies on physical and mental habits, which should include

- maintaining unwavering self-belief,
- having a winning attitude (exemplified by the player who commits for the full 90 minutes, never losing but simply running out of time),
- focusing only on what he or she can control,
- showing the discipline to do the job,

© Mark Thompson/ALLSPORT

Control over your opponent includes courage to take risks when the game demands it.

- managing anger and mistakes ("staying in the green" as described in chapter 3),
- being able to forget the bad moments and having the resilience to bounce back,
- having the courage to take a risk when the situation demands it, and
- enjoying the satisfaction of competition.

Halftime

After 45 minutes comes a wonderful period that allows players to absorb the lessons of the first half and recompose their mental and emotional state in preparation for the second half. Players should develop a miniroutine to stay focused despite the sometimes overemotional atmosphere engendered by coaches.

Postgame

We recognize the postgame as a time for physical warm-down, but we may not use it effectively for mental and emotional calming. Players and coaches must handle victory or defeat in a way that provides for evaluation and learning but does not damage players' self-belief or self-esteem, which could produce future fear instead of confidence.

Scunthorpe Shocked out of Complacency!

One day I received a telephone call from Mark Lillis, the coach of Scunthorpe United, a Division 3 team. After winning a tough cup-tie away from home, Scunthorpe had been drawn in the next round at home to the only nonleague team left in the competition. Lillis immediately recognized that his players' state of mind had moved into the comfort zone of complacency, and he understood how dangerous this could be when playing a team with nothing to lose and everything to gain.

Mark acted on my advice and persuaded the local newspaper to print two versions of the sports page that would report the Cup game. For the week preceding the game Mark covered the wall of the dressing room and nearby corridors (plus the inside of all toilet doors) with the report that Scunthorpe had won easily and drawn Manchester United at Old Trafford in the next round. It was pure heaven for the players!

On the day of the game Mark replaced all the posters with the second version of the newspaper report—one that recounted how Scunthorpe embarrassingly lost to the nonleaguers and missed the chance to play at Old Trafford—pure hell! The effect on the players was dramatic. Shocked out of their complacency, they changed their pregame approach sufficiently to prepare them physically and mentally to win the cup-tie.

Don Shula (1995), the successful American football coach, had this philosophy about handling the postgame period:

> When we win we know it is not final—we know we've got to line up next week and prove ourselves all over again. If we lose, we also know we're not dead, and we must get off the floor and have a chance to change the score next time we play.

Players must find, as in the examples above, a way of dealing with the postgame passion and moving on to a calm perspective of their performance—a personal evaluation. When they have dealt with the formalities and found their space, they might ask themselves these questions:

- How do I feel about today?
- What did I learn?
- Did I achieve my personal goals?
- What obstacles stood in my way?
- Did I get in the way of my own performance?
- Do I need a discussion with the coach or sports psychologist?
- Do I need to amend my routines for pregame and halftime?
- What is my personal action plan to prepare for the next game?

Whatever the postgame strategy, the most important point is that it ends with the player looking forward to the next game.

Summary

The challenge for players will always come at game time when their ability and character will be fully put to the test. Players must overcome their fear of failure and seek peak competitiveness by thorough and holistic physical, technical, tactical, and emotional preparation.

Players can achieve the ideal performance state, or flow, only by making a commitment to a healthy lifestyle, developing a strong work ethic, and having a willingness to develop good mental and emotional skills through repeated practice. The psychological quick fix doesn't exist. Players must also develop effective routines for match day.

In the end players rely on good physical and mental habits to ensure their competitiveness and control during games. They can most easily attain the ideal performance state by having the trust to relax mentally and let habits take over.

chapter

8

Communication

Sharing Information Effectively

**Flatter me, and I may not believe you.
Criticise me, and I may not like you.
Ignore me, and I may not forgive you.
Encourage me, and I will not forget you.**

William Arthur Ward

The England youth team sat in silence at the prematch meal before facing the Republic of Ireland, then the European champions, in Dublin. Looking at the players and noting the awkwardness of their body language, I realized that this team, which had assembled for the first time three days earlier, had developed neither relationships nor cohesion. The team had the feel of losers.

I broke the silence by asking Stephen Wright, a Liverpool player with a strong personality, to stand up and introduce everyone at his table to the rest of the room. Stephen struggled through in an embarrassed silence. I then gave every table two minutes to prepare before I went around the room asking other players the same question.

What followed, of course, was a buzz of activity, communication, and energy as each player made sure he knew everyone's name. In stages, I increased the difficulty of the task ("Tell me everybody at the table over there," "Identify the three players from Everton," and so on.) In the end, and I included the staff, everybody was talking, the room became alive, and we had made a step toward developing team chemistry. We left for the game in a happy, confident, energetic state, and the players maximized on their ability to win 5-0.

If this book helps to develop a more complete player and coach by involving them in the wider issues of mental, emotional, and lifestyle aspects of performance, then to a great extent it will depend on extending the language of soccer and the ability of players and coaches to communicate effectively in these new terms.

Soccer has always had its own language covering physical and technical performance—the simple language of command and response. But soccer in the year 2000 has become more complex and sophisticated. Players are better educated and more independent. The coach today will have to deal with all this to create a cohesive team that meets all challenges.

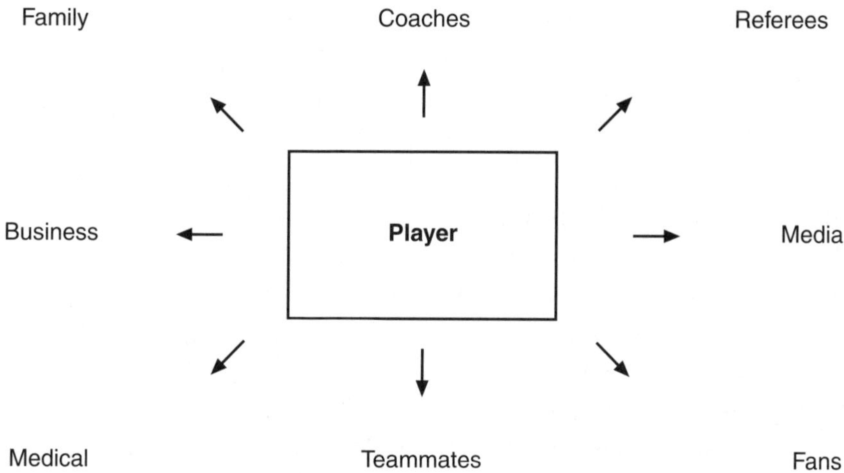

Figure 8.1 The player and communication.

Communication, in all forms and modes, has begun an inexorable rise to the top of the agenda, and a coach or player without the ability to give and receive the information necessary for the highest levels of performance will suffer. Figures 8.1 and 8.2 illustrate the demands placed on players and coaches to be effective communicators. They must be able to interact successfully with a variety of people in a range of styles and situations.

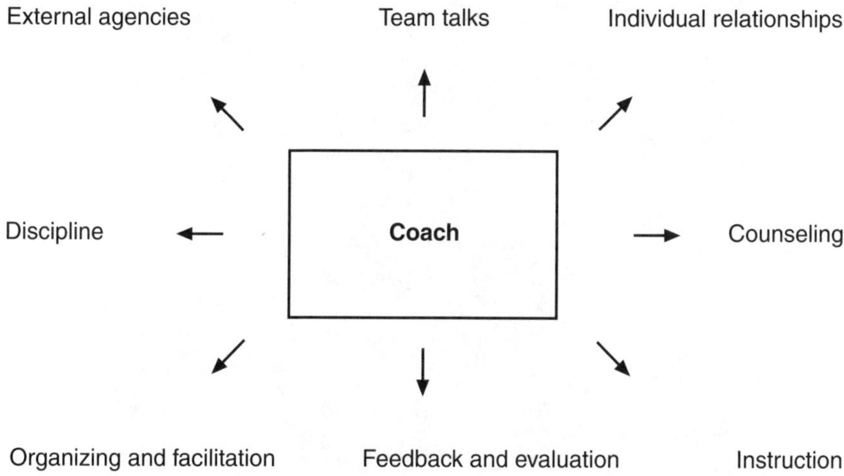

Figure 8.2 Responsibilities of a coach dependent on communication skill.

The extended language of soccer by which players and coaches will transmit their thoughts and feelings will involve several modes:

- Self-talk—players should recognize the importance of disciplining the inner voice to stay positive.
- Verbal—the majority of soccer interactions occur on the move, and verbal dexterity can be important to success.
- Listening—a major shift for coaches, and some players, will be recognizing the need to develop good listening skills.
- Connecting—communicating beyond technical needs can build personal relationships—coach-player bonds and player-player bonds—that can build team chemistry.
- Body language—it is not just what is said but also the way it is expressed that communicates the complete message. Coaches, in particular, must be careful that their body language does not betray them.

Body language helps to communicate the complete message.

• Visual—most players can retain no more than three points that a coach might make orally. A list on a flip chart or a poster on the dressing-room wall, however, might help players absorb more detail by allowing them to return to the message several times.

• Technological—the modern player is accustomed to receiving messages sent technologically, and coaches must become familiar with these new opportunities—audiotape, videos, e-mails, and so on—to stimulate and educate.

Clearly, the coach or player must communicate in a way that suits his or her personality and philosophy. But coaches and players should recognize that they can learn the skills required of all forms of communication. Such efforts can bring worthwhile rewards.

Principles of Good Communication

No matter what the context, some fundamental principles of communication are essential knowledge for both players and coaches:

- Know and use the other person's name. This is both courteous and relaxing.
- Be prepared by knowing what you want the outcome to be.
- Be empathetic. Try to understand the viewpoint of the other person. The goal is to connect, not to defeat.
- Be relaxed and open—take care of negative body language.
- Face the person you are talking to and establish eye contact.
- Choose a style according to who you are talking to. Simple is usually best.
- Remain on agenda—don't become sidetracked.
- Be objective and control emotions.
- Be honest. Don't say one thing and mean another.
- Occasionally seek clarification that your message has been received and understood.
- Repeat key messages. Find alternate ways to emphasize them.
- Lighten things up whenever possible with a little humor.
- Allow time for questions.
- Listen attentively using good body language.

- Try to understand and make allowance for different cultures.
- In concluding the conversation, try to sum up what has been agreed on.

Breakdowns in Communication

By understanding barriers to communication, coaches and players may be able to prevent some of them from occurring. Listed here are typical incidents I have witnessed in which the process of communication has failed:

- Assumptions—coaches assume players know what is required of them, and players assume that coaches know how they feel.
- Differences of opinion—although unavoidable, differences must lead to more communication, not less. Parties should agree to disagree.
- Personality clashes—this too is inevitable, but with communication a common ground can be established so that personal issues can be put aside for team needs.
- Role conflicts—players will resent playing in roles that do not fit their perception of their best contribution, but coaches can ease matters by sharing their reasons. Perhaps a consensus can be reached. Uncertainty of roles and expectations will create a defensive climate within a team.
- Power struggles—teams are always evolving, and the pecking order will always be considered important. Unless the head coach or team captain settles this by clear and shared communication, matters will only deteriorate.
- Cultural misunderstandings—great care must be taken to recognize and understand culturally influenced communication. Coaches must consider the words they use and their body language in expressing their message. They should always check that the players are clear on what they have said.
- Perceived injustices—soccer often requires instant decision making, producing many opportunities for conflict. Coaches must always have the power to make such decisions, and the players must have the discipline to carry them out. At the same time, it would be beneficial to have in place a feedback process that releases tension rather than builds it.

• Role changes—events occur every day in professional clubs (nonselection, injury, loss of form) that force players into role changes and possible loss of status. A rapid decline in communication often follows, thereby exacerbating the problem. Coaches and players must be sensitive to this and find ways of maintaining supportive communication.

Creating a Communication Network

In reviewing my three years of consultancy at Derby County, I feel that my major contribution was moving the club from a defensive climate of communication—cliques, power struggles, detachment of some individuals from the group, personal attacks instead of performance criticism—to a supportive climate with positive communication and a shared ownership of the issues facing the team.

With teams at the level of Derby County the quantity and quality of interaction will always fluctuate as team membership changes—new faces, new cultures—but certain measures helped accommodate the shifts and maintain a positive climate:

• Honesty—we always try for clear, consistent, direct communication that is honest and contains no hidden agendas. The criterion is that if it's what is best for the team, we have no problem sharing it.

• Feedback—players need constant feedback. Our coaches spend a great deal of time preparing instruction and comments for the players.

• Stability—too many changes can upset the mental and emotional stability of the team, increasing anxiety and decreasing communication. At Derby we have constant discussion about the benefit of stability against the advantage of change.

• Continuity of selection—being on the team is important for every player. Generally, a squad of players comes to terms with who is likely to be on the team and who is not. Although change will always occur, at Derby we regard a high level of continuity as the key to maintaining positive attitudes and communication—and therefore performance.

• Core and fringe—every team is likely to have core players, continuous selections who carry much of the responsibility, and fringe players who are not yet regulars. Although we do not ignore fringe players, at Derby we have a policy of prioritizing communication with our core players. The head coach will see them as a group once in a while, and the captain will meet with me once every week. This provides us with early warning signals and helps us understand the mood of the dressing room and avoid conflict.

• Team talks—to help the players (and coaches) make the transition from home to work, players start the day in our famous Prozone room, where specialized chairs pump sound waves through their bodies to stimulate blood supply and ensure a thorough warm-up. Starting this way also offers the benefit of being able to communicate with the whole squad and staff at a fixed time. We use the time to begin focus, receive administrative and organizational details, review past games, and discuss future games. I have time to make presentations influencing the players' mental and emotional state.

• Video—the use of video, the most natural form of communication for some of our modern players, has increased dramatically at Derby. We can now create our own videos and target them for motivational or educational purposes. It is often true that a key image has more impact than a thousand words.

• Focus groups—for particular issues, for example, the play of the goalkeeper and the back three defenders (we play 3-5-2), the coaches will not hesitate to meet with only the players concerned, holding a discussion supported by video evidence. Similarly, I may conduct a team-building exercise in which we agree on our team goals for the next season. Such agreements will form the basis for further discussion during the season.

• One on one—at the end of the day, soccer is a personal challenge. The most important communication in a club are the one-to-one discussions between coach and coach, coach and player, and player and player. These need not be formalized; players often feel more comfortable when they happen in an informal context. Coaches must seek these contact moments, taking care to seek out all players, not just the stars. Some coaches record such interactions to ensure that they do not ignore anyone for too long. I have found this to be the best way of learning the needs, hopes, and goals of each player.

Getting Feedback During a Crisis

In one of Derby County's bad spells the manager, Jim Smith, became frustrated because the players would not respond to his demands for their views of the situation. I explained to Jim that in an open situation like a team meeting with players from several different countries, it was unlikely that players would respond to such a challenge.

As always, Jim agreed to let me intervene. At the end of the afternoon team meeting, all the staff left and I was alone with the team. After offering some relaxing humor, I explained to the players that it was in their interests to provide feedback. I offered to organize it in a confidential, nonthreatening manner.

I divided the players into five groups, and added a Spanish-Italian interpreter to one. I asked them to list on paper at least five ways the club could break out of its run of poor form. Because I asked that no names appear on the sheets, I could reassure the boys that this was a confidential exercise. Much of my relationship with the players is based on trust, so this posed no problem.

I expected a 10-minute session, but the players so appreciated the opportunity to share their feelings that I finally had to end the exercise after 45 minutes. At a coaches' meeting later that afternoon, I listed all of the players' suggestions. We decided we would implement nine of them, with four put in place for the next day's practice. The reaction of the boys the next day was tremendous. They had been heard and responded to, and the whole atmosphere improved with everybody pulling together.

Unfortunately, we couldn't implement the best suggestion, which concerned our young play-anywhere star, Rory Delap: "Clone Rory 11 times!"

Communication and the Player

Soccer is a team game played in a social setting. No player can remain isolated from the variety of external pressures to communicate. As always with pressure, the player has the choice of avoiding challenge, coping with it, or thriving on it. Rick Pitino (1997) says in his book *Success Is a Choice* that players have no choice because if they can't communicate they won't be successful. He goes on to say that those who can communicate will benefit: "Communication is about making contact with others who can help you achieve your goals—and you in turn can help them achieve theirs."

As players reach higher levels, the problems that can destroy progress—nonselection, injury, loss of form, change of clubs, personal and family problems, and so on—become more significant. Communication is the only way to start solving these problems. The player needs to have the courage and confidence to seek help. My role with both England and Derby County is to ensure that no player becomes isolated. I am "everybody's friend" and often the first point of contact.

Players may wish to follow these guidelines:

- Build a positive support group—people you know you can go to who will listen and help.
- Listen and learn from criticism—accept it as part of developing excellence.
- Be open with teammates and become part of a supportive network of communication. Botterill and Patrick (1996) offer this logic:

> Supporting and encouraging teammates under pressure is one of the most important elements of effective expressiveness. It has a tremendous effect on people's feelings of readiness, confidence, and motivation, and usually produces a reciprocal response that is both valuable and rewarding.

- Develop good listening powers—you can learn from everyone.
- Learn to maintain communication in emotional situations.
  - Cope with the give and take of the club.
  - Deal with the difficult issues in an open, straightforward way.
  - Share information.
  - Accept the bad news as readily as the good.

Communication and the Team

When a sports psychologist investigates problems within a team, he or she searches for hot spots through questioning and observation. In most cases, the hot spots are communication problems.

Typical problem situations include the following:

- Conflict being managed badly
- Cultural differences, especially with the talented Caribbean players
- Coach intimidation
- The coach not listening so players feel their problems are not being dealt with
- Channels of communication being mixed up

TABLE 8.1 COMMUNICATION FOR BUILDING TEAM CHEMISTRY

THE COACH	THE TEAM-BUILDING PROCESS	THE PLAYER
Inspire	The coach sells the vision	Listen
Listen	Players buy in to the vision	Commit
Discuss	Team's operating procedures and shared ownership agreed to in discussion	Discuss and question
Accept as a role model	Team values and identity confirmed by consensus	Accept as a role model
Clarify	Review the process so far	Understand
Challenge	Set team goals	Accept
Appreciate individual	Set individual goals	Be open and assertive
Be positive	Hard work, support, encouragement	Be positive
Be constructive, not personal	Instruction, challenge, evaluation, and feedback	Listen attentively
Control emotions	Mistake management and correction	Understand and accept
Praise	Reward and reinforce good play	Enjoy
Conduct meetings	Maintain flow of information	Maintain awareness
Seek player enjoyment	Humor eases; worry prolongs	Contribute to enjoyment
Be open—fair but firm	Apply discipline when necessary	Accept and move on
Offer empathy	Deal with players' lifestyle problems	Seek help
Keep communicating	Handle the bad times	Keep communicating
Increase communication	Resolve conflicts	Increase communication
Listen and respect	Support players' individual needs at competition time	Be assertive to control situation

Some tension and anxiety is inevitable in a team striving to achieve, but the only way to relieve this is to increase communication and the feeling of shared ownership of the problems.

Chapter 10 examines the building of team cohesion and the role of effective and regular communication. Table 8.1 highlights this by emphasizing the communication elements necessary for both coach and players in building team chemistry. In each step of the team-building process, the communication responsibilities for coaches and players are identified.

Communication Icebreaker

For teams assembled with players from different clubs or teams that have recruited several new players, I have a favorite ice-breaking game that encourages shared communication in a nonthreatening and enjoyable way.

The players all sit in a circle, and the captain holds a ball. I inform them that on a flip chart I have written several questions, each on a separate page, that I want them to answer. The captain starts. After answering, he or she throws the ball to someone else in the circle, who repeats the process. Each question will be shown for only three minutes, and then I will flip over to the next question.

The trick is to start with nonthreatening questions and then slowly move the team to issues I really want them to debate. Here are the questions I used when working with a women's soccer team that had some team cohesion problems:

Q1. The best thing about playing soccer is . . .
Q2. The worst thing about playing soccer is . . .
Q3. The team I admire most is . . . because . . .
Q4. The team that disappoints me most is . . . because . . .
Q5. The player I admire most is . . . because . . .
Q6. The player who disappoints me most is . . . because . . .
Q7. The teammate I admire most is . . . because . . .
Q8. The three key things I can offer this team are . . .
Q9. This team would do better if . . .

In this simple half-hour exercise, the questions can be varied to focus the communication on the team's specific problems. In such a fast-moving exercise, a high degree of honesty and disclosure often occurs.

Communication and the Coach

Communication is the first step to success for every coach. As Bill Parcells (1995) puts it, "Coaching is an act of communication—of explaining what you want of people in a way that allows them to do it."

My observation of coaches, often ex-players, working at the highest levels identifies three major communication issues:

1. Coaches allow their emotions to become involved when watching games. They become spectators rather than analytical observers. They fail to note some of the important points that might help their teams. Halftime, then, may become an expression of emotion rather than objective communication targeted on winning the game.

2. Coaches have little training in communication. Most do not use the power of the flip chart or video, for example. One of the ways to avoid the boredom of repeating important messages is to vary the format. If the coach is talented technically but communicates poorly, it makes sense to use a skilled assistant or a sports psychologist to take the lead occasionally in team talks or individual counseling.

3. Coaches often become so wrapped up in the process of teaching soccer that they forget that people are involved. An example of such ineffective communication was quoted in the Football Coaches Association journal in which Leif Isberg (1997) monitored the instructions that youth coaches gave to players. In three matches, coaches sent 116, 187, and 55 messages to players to change behavior. Isberg classified 67, 55, and 12 as redundant because the coaches failed to use a player's name, which produced uncertainty.

Some useful guidelines for coaches include the following:

- All communication from the coach is important, so be sure that players cannot misinterpret your messages.
- Be proactive and communicate when you see a problem. Don't wait and hope it will go away.
- Use positive language that creates positive expectancies of the players. Challenge the players to be better rather than punishing them for being poor.
- Never assume.

- Make every communication seem important. Show respect to all players.
- Allow time for everybody. Research indicates that coaches spend far more time (up to seven times more!) with star players.
- Never promise anything you cannot deliver.
- Never threaten anything you cannot enforce.
- Be aware of body language when communicating. Lombardi (1996) reports a fascinating study by Mehrebian, who examined factors influencing coach-to-player communication. Only 7 percent of the impact was verbal (the words used), 38 percent of the impact was vocal (how the words were said), and 55 percent of the impact was nonverbal (the body language used).
- To reinforce players' self-esteem, balance praise with criticism (the sandwich technique is praise-criticism-praise). Tip the balance more toward praise with younger players whose self-esteem can be easily damaged.
- When communicating after a mistake, focus on the correction, not the mistake.
- Work on improving personal control of emotions.
- Learn to be a good listener.
- Learn to be a good questioner. Encourage players to self-reference, to assess themselves rather than always getting the coach's view. Ask, "How do you think you are doing?"
- Be aware of cultural differences and make allowances.
- Use players' names and know something of their families so you can express concern for them as people, not just players.
- Be prepared. Follow Steven Covey's (1989) advice in knowing what outcome you want: "Start with the end in mind."
- Criticize only performance, not the person.
- Avoid communicating when out of emotional control. Learn to wait for perspective and objectivity.
- Make maximum use of informal opportunities to communicate. A quiet word on the training ground often works better than a formal meeting.
- Use humor—fun is a great stress reliever.

- Always end communications by clarifying what you have agreed on: "So let's agree this is what we have decided to do."

Setting the Tone

Coaches should prepare for all meetings, but of special importance to the England teams is the first meeting, when the coach must establish ground rules, attitude, and spirit. Below is my advice to the head coach for the arrival-day meeting (45 minutes maximum):

- As the first significant team meeting, it will set the tone for both communication and relationships.
- Offer a friendly welcome but move straight into an authoritative, businesslike manner. You are selling your confidence and expertise.
- Insist from the start that the team concentrate, listen, and show respect for whoever is speaking (permit no mobile telephones).
- If possible arrange a comfortable room with no distractions where players can all sit in a circle. This facilitates eye contact and indicates equal responsibility.
- Get any initial or potential problems out into the open to begin with, so players can listen with a clear mind. For example, ask, "Any problems with the rooms? Any problems with the food? Any health problems? Any other issues? OK, now we can begin."
- Reintroduce your staff and indicate that each will speak for a few minutes after you have finished.
- Whenever possible use players' names. Tell them what you and the staff wish to be called. Identify clearly the team's task and define what you will consider success. Remind the staff and players that they can only succeed through each other, that everybody is important. Share your vision of the way things should go. Offer a simple, clear, positive message that everyone can commit to.
- Remind players why they were selected and that they have a responsibility to live up to that honor. Indicate the standards, on and off the field, that are integral to any team.

- Review the obstacles that might prevent success.
- Talk the players through the preparation program (a visual aid and handouts of the schedule for the players will help). Gain their acceptance for the direction you intend to take them to ensure success.
- Ask if players have any questions so far. Listen carefully to any questions or comments.
- Talk openly and honestly about the things that directly or indirectly can affect team progress.
- Always use the word "we" to emphasize the shared nature of the exercise.
- Remind everyone of past success and the role that the experienced players in the group can play in helping the new players.
- End this first phase by reminding players of your vision of the way things should go.
- Introduce each member of the staff in turn and let them explain their roles in no more than two minutes each.
- Show a motivational video. We used *This Is England,* a short reprise of the national team's greatest moments.
- Conclude by linking the "best practice" of the video to your high expectations for this team.

Summary

Soccer is an increasingly sophisticated team game in which the ability to communicate effectively is vital to successful players and cohesive teams. Players and coaches need training not only in the traditional verbal and nonverbal skills of communication but also in the use of modern technology. In either case, the objective is to transmit and receive messages that improve understanding of the game and the players' particular roles.

When problems at soccer clubs are investigated, it is often the case that communication has broken down. Players and coaches are urged to increase, not decrease, communication in times of crisis. Fundamental to team chemistry is relationship building. Effective communication is a crucial element in developing team cohesion.

chapter
9

Role Definition

Playing Within the Team Framework

There is no greater waste of a resource than that of unrealized talent.

President Franklin Roosevelt

One of the saddest sights in English soccer was the television report of the expulsion of Paul Gascoigne from the England pre-World Cup 1998 training camp. Paul, the most technically gifted player in the squad, could not come to terms with certain emotional and lifestyle issues and broke the rules that bound the squad together.

Biographies of coaches often highlight a relationship between a coach and a talented player who had difficulty fitting into a team framework. Coach Phil Jackson refused to let Dennis Rodman's lifestyle—he occasionally turned up for games wearing a dress—distract him from persuading Rodman to do his main job of winning rebounds for the Chicago Bulls. He rationalized (Halberstam 1999) that "every tribe of Indians has a backward walking member," and urged the rest of the team to show maturity and professionalism in dealing with their contrary teammate.

Similarly, the successful rugby coach Carwyn James dealt with the great Barry John's dislike of training by letting him play soccer with the local children while on tour in New Zealand.

Although this book attempts to paint the picture of the complete player, it acknowledges the difficulty of finding players with all the gifts—physical, technical, mental, and emotional—who are willing to live a supportive lifestyle. To be successful, coaches must deal with less talented players and not allow weaknesses to get in the way of strengths.

At a recent workshop, I asked the coaches to rank the 20 English Premier League teams in order of player talent. Derby County was ranked 18th, and team X was ranked 4th. I compared this ranking to the final league placings. Derby finished 8th, and team X finished 14th—a difference of 10 places for each team. Clearly, Derby overachieved because the coaching staff had a positive influence on flawed players, whereas team X needs to review their coaching staff and procedures.

International teams do not have time to change flawed players and must always compromise to get the most out of what each player can contribute. We have learned that players fall into high-

TABLE 9.1 CHARACTERISTICS OF HIGH- AND LOW-MAINTENANCE PLAYERS

HIGH MAINTENANCE	LOW MAINTENANCE
Extrinsically motivated, needs constant stroking	Intrinsically motivated, does not seek attention
Undisciplined, not trustworthy	Disciplined, trustworthy
Ego-driven, focused on self	Task-driven, focused on performance
Sees problems, not challenges	Sees challenges, not problems
Struggles when the team dips	Survives when the team dips
Tries to do the jobs of others	Knows and does own job
Can't let mistakes go	Recovers from mistakes
Inconsistent performer	Consistent performer
Needs standards to be set	Sets own standards
Gives problems off the pitch	Causes no problem off the pitch

maintenance and low-maintenance categories (see table 9.1). We cannot afford to have too many high-maintenance players in a group with only a few days to prepare for a major game.

Good coach-player relationships do not occur by accident. Building them requires time, effort, and planning. Derby's success has been its ability to create a working environment in which everyone has a clear understanding and appreciation of both his own role and the role of others in helping the team win.

Defining a Player's Role

The individual player will feel ready to play only by understanding his or her job on the pitch and by accepting that role.

Role clarity and acceptance is a major part of building a player's confidence and motivation and integrating that player into a team unit. Players can check how well they are doing by asking themselves these questions:

- Do I enjoy my role?
- Do I know what's expected of me in all circumstances?

- Am I still learning new things?
- Do the coaches still stimulate me?
- Do I have to be at my best to stay on this team?

If this is all happening, the player will feel fully engaged in his or her role and be motivated to master new challenges, thus being almost in a state of flow. When it is not happening, when practice is routine and nonchallenging, the player will become stale, lose motivation and focus, and make critical mistakes.

The responsibility of the coach is to ensure mental clarity and emotional balance by preparing players for their roles in empathetic, interesting, and challenging ways. Good coaches reduce complexity for players. Bill Walsh (1998) describes coaching as "the reduction of uncertainty."

Although all positions share certain fundamental requirements, coaches must be able to teach special skills and responsibilities for various positions. If the player knows that the coach has a real understanding of his or her position, the player will be far more willing to accept criticism of performance. This will maintain a good coach-player relationship.

One of the ways I have promoted this is to suggest that coaches prepare job descriptions of each player's role and responsibilities within the particular tactical shape of the team. Table 9.2 provides an outline of the profile and skills of a central midfield player acting as a front sweeper in front of a back line of three defenders. This description would help both player and coach understand the role and would provide a way to assess strengths and weaknesses.

Michelle Akers, a leading player on the USA women's world championship team, demands such analysis and attention to detail from her coaches:

> Coaches must extend women players as much as the guys. It's no good telling a girl "well done," when she's lost control and trapped the ball a few yards out in front of her. I divide my goals into the following categories—fitness, technique, mental, position-specific and diet.

Another advantage of having job descriptions is that coaches can more easily recognize mismatches between role demands and player abilities. Darren Edmundson at Carlisle was a failing midfield player, a clear mismatch, until it was recognized that his abilities

TABLE 9.2 SAMPLE JOB DESCRIPTION

For a central midfield player acting primarily as a sweeper in front of a back line of three defenders

ELEMENT	CHARACTERISTICS
Physical	Strong physical presence, intimidating, durable (doesn't become injured easily), good stamina, quick over short distances, can jump to win headers, outstanding work ethic
Technical	Excellent quick control (always playing in traffic), can pass short with high certainty and long with accuracy, can join the attack and has good long shot, understands that simplicity is excellence for this role
Mental	Good learner, quick thinker, decisive, tough minded, highly disciplined, resilient (recovers from mistakes), accepts responsibility, outstanding concentration, intelligent reader of game situations
Emotional	Calm, composed presence at heart of the team, excellent self-control and good at leading teammates, never intimidated or provoked, deals with stress well, trustworthy, potential captain
Lifestyle	Dedicated athlete with lifestyle to match, will not abuse body, conscientious about game preparation, does not seek glory or headlines

matched those of a fullback. He became a strong player at his new position. Similarly, Sir Geoff Hurst, scorer of a hat trick in the 1966 World Cup final, was converted from a failing midfield player into a world-class striker.

In this age of video analysis and improved statistical information, it is easier for coaches and players to match the job description to the actual performance, improve the quality of feedback, and agree on a relevant practice program.

Tables 9.3 and 9.4 show how far the coaches at Derby County—in this case Coach Steve Round, assisted by our most experienced coach, Billy McEwan—go to provide each player with the best possible analysis of his performance and progress in his specific job. Table 9.3 concerns overall player performance, and table 9.4 examines psychological performance. Each player would also receive similar assessments of technical performance and game appreciation, with the charts indicating where he can best achieve improvement.

At the end of every season, the Derby County coaches challenge the players to review their roles and job descriptions and identify how they are going to improve 10 percent the next season. Then I challenge the coaches to do the same.

School of Excellence

Reference **5**
Forename **Danny**
Surname **Porter**
Team **Pro**
Birth Date **23 January 1979**
Position **LB/CB**

Derby County Football Club

Date	Time	Category	Assessor	Assessor total	Player total	Total difference
1 May 1999	12:00:00	Player performance	Billy McEwan	32	40	-8

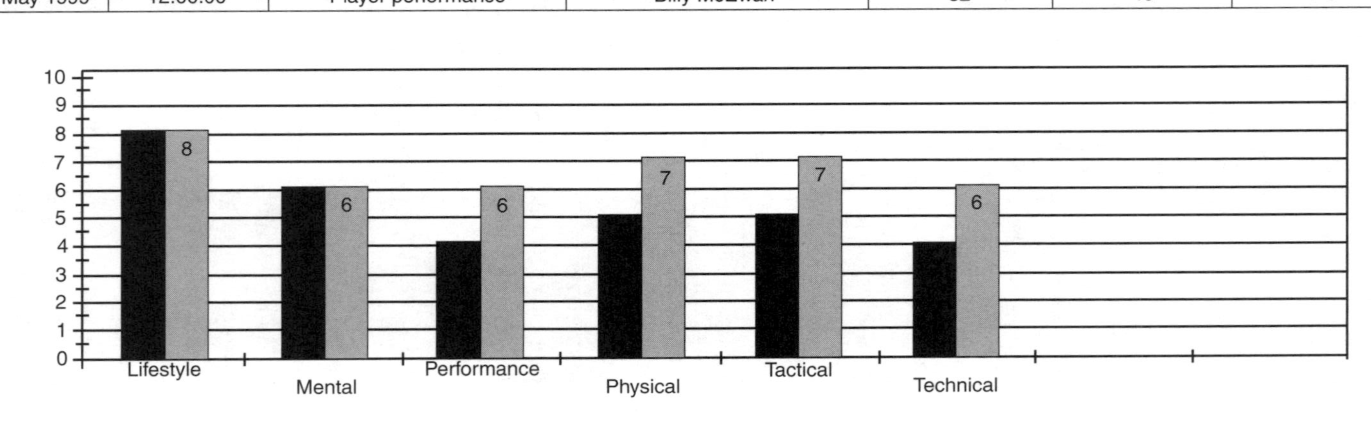

Table 9.3 Player assessment chart—performance.

School of Excellence

Reference	**5**
Forename	**Danny**
Surname	**Porter**
Team	**Pro**
Birth Date	**23 January 1979**
Position	**LB/CB**

Derby County Football Club

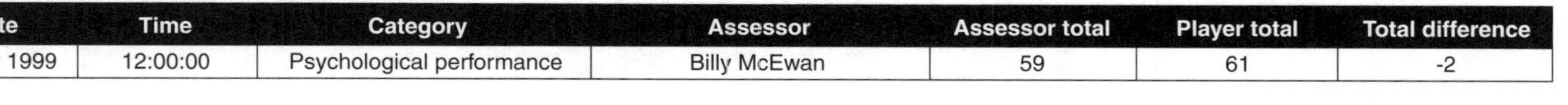

Date	Time	Category	Assessor	Assessor total	Player total	Total difference
1 May 1999	12:00:00	Psychological performance	Billy McEwan	59	61	-2

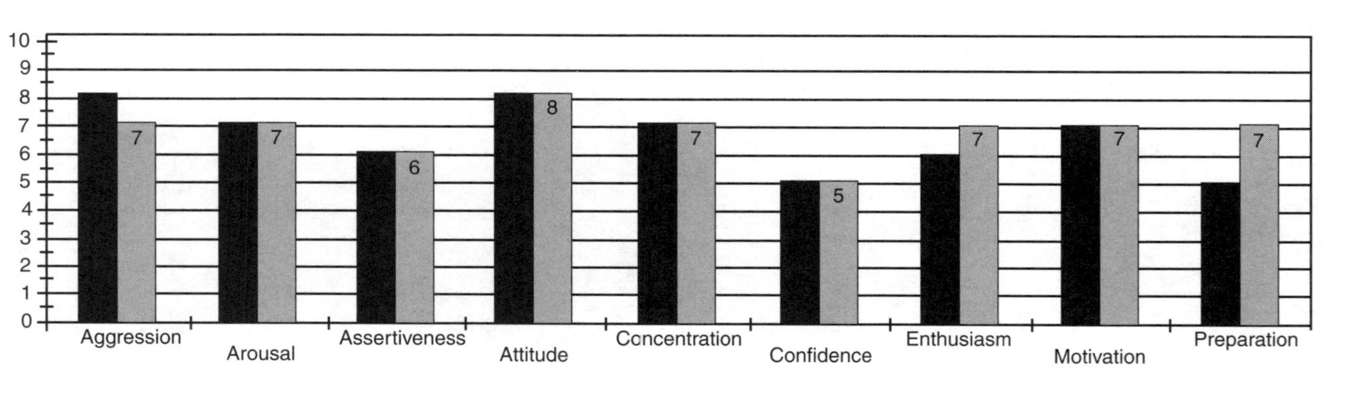

Table 9.4 Player assessment chart—psychological.

Human Beings or Human Doings?

The process of establishing role clarity, acceptance, and accountability can only evolve by the coach and player working together. This book has encouraged the democratizing of the coach-player relationship. When the player and coach share an understanding of the player's role, several benefits will become evident:

- Communication increases and anxiety decreases.
- The player feels that his or her experience and knowledge are valued.
- The player understands his or her strengths and weaknesses.
- The player self-references and takes responsibility for his or her performance.
- The danger of asking the player to do things beyond his or her capability is reduced.
- The player is accountable in a more objective manner, reducing the chance of unfair criticism from the coach.
- Mutual respect increases.

Thus the player and coach both have the critical information they need to do their jobs under the pressure and demands of the game. Just as important, shared ownership stimulates the player's emotional attachment to the team. A new player, or a disaffected player, who buys into the idea of shared ownership will naturally become integrated with the ambitions and structure of the team. Bill Walsh (1998) summarizes the process:

> By establishing his role on the team and taking pride in the fact he is contributing in a tangible way, a rookie can achieve a sense of control in his professional life. Not only is he able to earn his "keep," he is also able to acquire the acceptance of his teammates.

Ten Steps to Developing a Player's Ability to Perform a Role

Coaches can help players by establishing the right learning environment:

1. Create a job description. Decide what the player must learn in order to do his or her job superbly, assessing the job demands as described in table 9.2.

2. Assess the player. How does the player's present level of physical, technical, mental, and emotional capacity fit the requirements of the job? Identify the weaknesses that require special attention.

3. Design relevant practice. Apart from the general work every player needs, what does this player especially need to practice for this particular job?

4. Bias practice for success. Lead the player forward in a series of small, manageable steps that create an atmosphere of success and show the player that training pays off.

5. Give criticism with care. The player will need ongoing evaluation (coaching is the reduction of errors), but it must be positive and productive, encouraging the player to deal with mistakes and criticism as a necessary part of the learning process.

6. Treat setbacks as part of the journey. If it were easy, everybody would play soccer well. But it isn't, so the player must be prepared for setbacks. The coach must retain emotional control and focus on the learning process and error reduction. The clever coach will use such errors as a guide to prepare for future practices, thereby ensuring relevance.

7. Share ownership with the player. If the player feels involved from the start of the process, it is more likely that he or she will find the commitment to see it through to the end. The coach must encourage the player to share views. Both must be willing to deal with bad news as well as good.

8. Use "best practice" models. Players often learn easier and faster if they have a role model to emulate. Young players who watch a star player on video playing just the way the coach wants them to play are soon convinced. Similarly, a coach may take a player to a game so that both of them can concentrate on and learn from the play of a role model. For example, they might watch the player's work rate and contribution without the ball.

9. Reward progress. Coaches must look for players doing things right and reward any sign of improvement. The only way to create good habits is by constant repetition. To provide repetition without boredom, the coach must vary practice. The player needs the constant encouragement of both the coach and his or her social support group, avoiding any cynics and moaners among family and friends.

10. Evaluate progress. Players must see that they are improving

if they are to stay motivated, so coaches should seek any measures available to do this. These might include the following:

- Objective statistics—for example, the number of "clean sheets" for a goalkeeper
- Subjective reports—a compilation of the player's view, the coach's view, and the views of independent experts
- Video evidence—documentation that the player can see for himself or herself
- External approval—promotion to a higher team, selection for the national team, or media recognition

Role Within Teams

In a team game like soccer, players must do more than simply understand and perform their individual roles—they must do so within a cohesive pattern of 11 players either attacking or defending at any particular stage of the game. For advanced tactical systems—for example, the "total soccer" of former Holland teams—players may be asked to interchange positions.

The successful team player must take four steps in developing his or her particular role:

1. Understand and perform his or her role as a primary contribution to the team.
2. Form a unit with the players who play nearby and perform in coordination with them. This is sometimes known as teams within teams.
3. Understand the tactical shape of the whole team and how his or her particular role contributes to team success.
4. Be willing to accept any amendments to the role that the coaches determine necessary to win a particular game.

As these steps unfold, the coach might find the player resistant to change. The coach will have to employ more skills to reorient the player from personal goals to team goals. Occasionally I like to quote to the England youth team from Rudyard Kipling's second *Jungle Book:*

Now this is the Law of the Jungle
As old and as true as the sky

And the wolf that keeps it may prosper
And the wolf that shall break it must die

As the creeper that circles the tree trunk
The Law runneth forward and back
The strength of the pack is the wolf
And the strength of the wolf is the pack.

We have found symbols like this useful in encouraging togetherness and the concept that the team is the hero. Blending players' roles and responsibilities into a cohesive team is not easy. The case study "Soldier or Artist?" (page 136) tries to illustrate the varied nature of players and what each can offer if the coach can identify an appropriate role. Soldier-artists or artist-soldiers are relatively easy to fit within the team concept, but pure soldiers or pure artists can give the coach headaches. If the coach-player relationship is sound, however, then a role might be shaped that the player can accept and, just as important, that the rest of the team can see as beneficial to their chances of success.

Making Players Accountable

When I was coach of the England men's basketball team, I decided to take an 18-year-old player, Joel Moore, to a tournament in Japan. My motives were long term rather than short term. Joel would soon become a great player, and I needed to give him as much experience of the international environment as I could, especially knowing that he had never before traveled abroad.

Although the senior players carried nearly all the responsibility for our performance, at the end of a close game against Japan I was forced to play Joel. Unfortunately, the game ended with Joel missing two fouls shots with England one point behind. As I followed my team off the court, I decided on a postgame strategy that dealt with the defeat without being too damaging to Joel.

When I entered the dressing room, the players were sitting silently in despair. None felt worse than Joel did, of course. In an abrupt voice I asked the captain, Paul Stimpson, to stand and tell everybody two mistakes he had made in the game. One by one I made the seniors account for two mistakes publicly and then sit down. Joel's turn came. He admitted to missing the two foul shots and sat down while the next player was being called. I finished by revealing two coaching mistakes I had made and emphasized that as a team we were all responsible for both victories and defeats.

The matter was now closed, and I felt I had succeeded in not destroying a young man's self-esteem and confidence. That evening back at the hotel I sent for Joel. I told him I was disappointed and challenged him to be better next time. He went on to play for England over 80 times. Coaches have great power but must use it sensitively when bringing players to account.

Soldier or Artist?

Dave Sexton, one of England's most distinguished coaches, once remarked that a soccer team includes soldiers and artists. When I had the opportunity to work alongside Coach Sexton, I questioned him further. He felt that all players could be identified somewhere along a continuum:

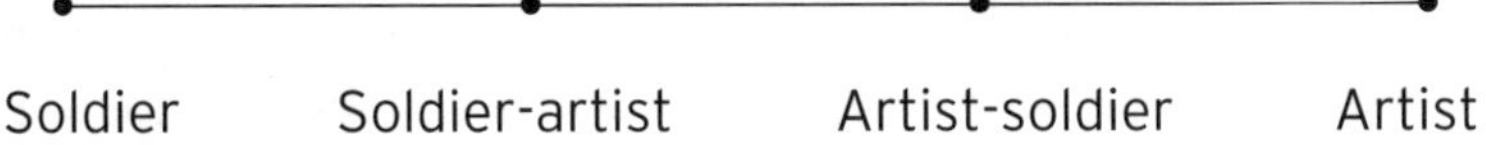

Soldier Soldier-artist Artist-soldier Artist

- The soldier was combative in nature, physically powerful, a natural defender or perhaps an abrasive attacker.
- The soldier-artist was similar to the soldier but with a touch of vision and skill that occasionally produced unexpected finesse.
- The artist-soldier was predominantly a player of vision and skill but could surprise everybody with the ability to compete strongly for the ball.
- The artist was a player of the highest skill levels, capable of making brilliant, insightful decisions on the pitch and forever seeking to make things happen.

Coach Sexton felt it was important for each player to know his or her natural style and what he or she could contribute. It was also important, Sexton believed, for the coach to place players in roles within a team shape that allowed them to express their talents.

Pure soldiers are easy to place in a role but will have limited ability to make a mark at the highest levels. Pure artists are prized but less easy to place in an efficient and effective role in competitive soccer played at the highest level.

For "total soccer" and the complete team, any coach would love a combination of soldier-artists and artist-soldiers, all of whom would find roles to suit them in a physically competitive team capable of moments of real skill and flair.

The Challenge Ahead

The process of coaching and getting players to play within the team framework is becoming more difficult. Rapid changes in society have created a different kind of player mentality—one that is typically more self-driven than team focused. Bill Walsh (1998) sums up this change:

> The "old school" represents such values as discipline, unquestioned authority, loyalty, accountability, and a willingness to sacrifice for the good of the team. The "new school," on the other hand, is more introspective. In other words, a "how does this matter affect my life" attitude has become a dominant factor in many issues.

Players now more often ask why. They demand greater ownership of their careers, and coaches must respond to a multifaceted agenda. In the professional game, team loyalty may cease to exist. Players at all levels will certainly move more often from club to club. Lifestyle issues will, unless managed, damage more players.

Players still strive to achieve their ambition, however, and will relate to a coach who can help them get there, a coach who spends time with them individually and has the expertise to help them do their jobs better and become more valuable members of a team. The challenge for the modern coach is to use persuasion, not domination.

Summary

To achieve a superior mental and emotional state, a player must completely understand the nature of his or her positional role. The coach can help the player identify and develop the necessary skills. By jointly developing a relevant job description and a program for improvement, the player and coach can make this process easier. Shared ownership of the process will enhance learning. Ten steps to creating a positive learning environment are described.

But a player cannot perform his or her role in isolation and must learn to fit into the team framework. The team must be the hero. Such integration can be challenging because the modern player's self-interest conflicts with team loyalty. The successful coach will offset this by persuading the player that only through the team can he or she achieve personal success in soccer.

chapter

10

Cohesion

Building a Unified Team

Peak performers are great "team" people. They care enough to encourage, challenge, and support teammates when necessary. They stay respectful and appreciative of the many "role" players and attributes that are necessary to create and maintain an effective team.

Michael Jordan

So far in this book we have built a picture of a complete soccer player with a foundation of physical ability and technical skills to which we have added mental and emotional skills. The final stage, as Michael Jordan suggests, is for the player to become a team player.

The player now must do more than synchronize all aspects of the body and mind. He or she must also be in tune with teammates and coaches. Only the team can win. Players must be able and willing to play their part in the sometimes painful and slow process of developing a coherent and successful team.

Every player will remember the moment when they walked into a new soccer club and confronted a collection of individuals of various backgrounds, abilities, and interests. They will recall that those players later became a group with a common purpose. The fortunate ones will have seen the group transform itself into a team with shared goals and a high degree of interdependency.

I say fortunate because I agree with Pat Riley (1993) that team building is not easy:

> Teamwork isn't simple. In fact, it can be a frustrating, elusive commodity. That's why there are so many bad teams out there, stuck in neutral or going downhill. Teamwork doesn't appear magically, just because someone mouths the words. It doesn't thrive just because of the presence of talent or ambition. It doesn't flourish simply because a team has tasted success.

Team building and teamwork occur only as the result of strategic development by an experienced coach and the voluntary commitment of players who are engaged and drawn in by the process. Both are essential to team success. Great teams are characterized by both the quality of leadership and the ability and commitment of the players.

B.W. Tuckman (1965) developed the classic analysis of the four steps to building a team:

1. Forming—individuals are gathered together and asked to commit to a common purpose.
2. Storming—as the coach shapes the team, tension and conflict develop as players compete for selection, specific roles, and status.
3. Norming—conflicts begin to be resolved, and players accept their roles and commit to the team identity.
4. Performing—the team is now achieving, highly unified in purpose and able to overcome problems and setbacks by working and staying together.

Each stage is a vital step toward the final, difficult stage of achieving effective performance while keeping a squad of players involved and committed. A final stage in the team's life cycle occurs when it ages and its performance diminishes. The coach will then have to re-form the team.

Team Stability—Mental and Emotional Issues

Having now experienced four seasons with a professional team in the most competitive soccer league in the world, I have witnessed all the stages of team building and the situations and incidents that conspire to destroy the process. The key to my work is establishing a mental and emotional stability that allows for consistent performance with the positive support of the players. Each week, the events of soccer—an unexpected loss, a key injury, the departure of a player, disagreements on selection, conflict between players, and so on—threaten the stability of the team and undermine its will to commit to the cause.

Daniel Goleman (1995) reinforces this:

> The single most important factor in maximising the excellence of a team's product was the degree to which the members were able to create a state of internal harmony—which let them take full advantage of the talents of their members.

Goleman suggested that factors acting negatively on the process of harmony were players who were either deadweights or dominators, players who couldn't cope with the give and take of a team, and the insidious effect of the emotions of fear, anger, rivalry, and resentment. Generally, in teams that lack cohesion everybody worries about people not doing their jobs.

Thus, the challenge of becoming a successful team member is far more likely to be emotional than it is physical. The soccer of tomorrow will require players to have basic skills of emotional intelligence so that they can play together effectively. To succeed in the toughest leagues and tournaments, teams will need to boost their collective emotional intelligence and achieve a high degree of stability.

Much of my work in preparing England teams for international play is directed at establishing the emotional intelligence and stability that allows physical skills to flourish in unfamiliar and difficult environments. Limited preparation time makes this difficult. Figure 10.1 shows my role in supporting and linking the

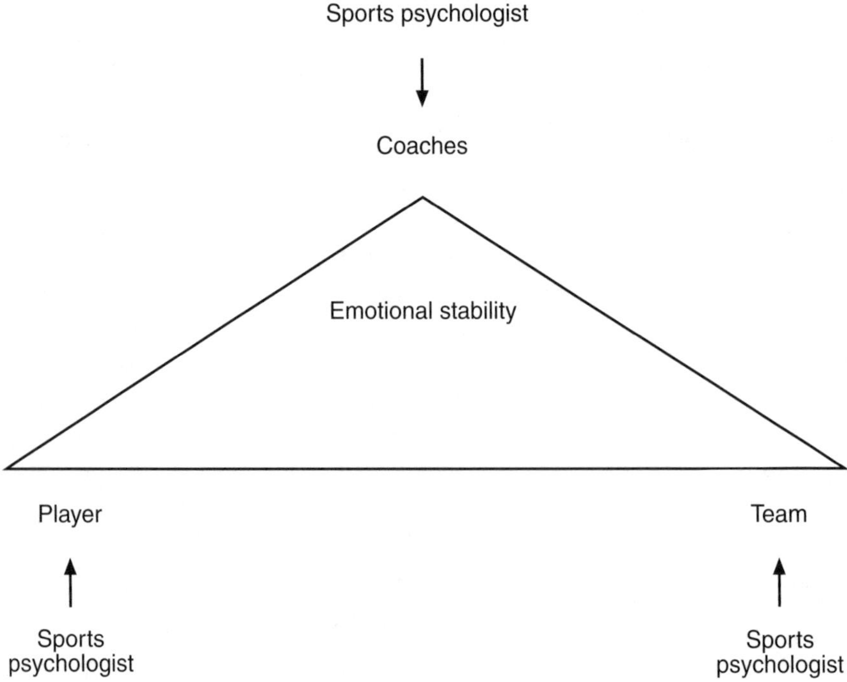

Figure 10.1 Sports psychologist's role in creating team emotional stability.

triangle of relationships by becoming everybody's friend. Because I know everybody's viewpoint, I can be proactive when stability is threatened by suggesting changes that defuse the situation. This echoes the belief of Ian McGeechan, coach of the successful British Lions rugby team on their tour of South Africa, who felt that if he got the psychology right everything else would fall into place.

Building Team Cohesion

Maintaining the psychological stability of a team at a good performance level throughout a long season or a challenging tournament is the result of the team's coherence, explained by Carron (1988) as "a dynamic process that is reflected in the tendency for a group to stick together and remain united in pursuit of its objectives and goals."

Such coherence in a team is built on two main foundations: task cohesion and social cohesion.

Task Cohesion

In teams with task cohesion, coaches and players agree on and understand the way the team intends to play. Each player is comfortable with his or her role. Lack of task cohesion could lead to problems in structure and coordination, communication and interaction, motivation, and concentration.

Social Cohesion

In teams with social cohesion, the players can relate and communicate with each other, are capable of solving problems, and can remain unified in identity and purpose. Lack of social cohesion could lead to problems of players who will not play together, will not play for each other, and will not bond together.

Building coherence is not easy because successful performance in highly competitive situations is a complex and fragile process requiring careful planning and patience. Sometimes teams that are not cohesive will win because of their talent, but this will not happen consistently. On the other hand, teams with less talent can often win games by maximizing the cohesive purpose and synergy of the team.

Successful performance requires a team to do many things right on a consistent and integrated basis. It is only through pursuing an active strategy of task and social cohesion that the coach can hope to achieve that. Similarly, players must examine their own qualities and ensure that they can be full and contributing members of such a process.

Building Team Cohesion on Tour

At my 1999 "Sports Psychology and Soccer" workshop I decided to invite four young coaches to present practical applications of sports psychology. Paul McGuinness, youth coaching coordinator at Manchester United, described how he built team cohesion on an under-12 team he took to an important tournament in Dallas. He decided on a five-step process that involved the coaches and players preparing together to build togetherness, discipline, and spirit:

1. The group watched the video of the British Lions rugby team on their successful tour of South Africa.
2. They decided together the aims of the tour.
3. They agreed on actions to achieve the aims.
4. The group discussed what quality leadership was and where and when they might need it.
5. Everybody agreed on the chain as a symbol of unity.

Paul explained that the shout of "Chain!" was a team-building strategy. Whenever this was called the squad had to group together in the positions they held on the pitch and hold onto each other tightly to form the links of a chain. Any of the staff or players could make the call anytime or anywhere. He chose the word "chain" to signify the following:

C Close gaps in the team—all work closely together.

H Hard to beat—individually and collectively.

A Attack the ball in your area and as a team.

I In position always—adjust as the ball moves.

N Never switch off, especially defensively.

If this worked, the group would become a team—**T**ogether **E**verybody **A**chieves **M**ore. The team did win the tournament. Paul felt that the chain strategy helped team cohesion in several ways:

- The group stayed switched on—during practice, at the hotel, at the airport.
- Individuals did not wander off from the group mentally or physically.
- Team spirit improved.
- The shout created an invigorating environment—the last one in the chain had to do press-ups (staff or boys).
- The team became different from the other teams and had a unique identity.
- The concept was a quick way to get everyone together.
- The physical contact created comfort and strength.
- The chain huddle before and after games strengthened team spirit.

TABLE 10.1 FORMING THE TEAM

Stage 1 Forming: a settling-in period

TASK COHESION	SOCIAL COHESION
• Good initial player recruitment will accelerate progress. • Staff should be selected for core job skills, skill in individual and team interaction, and problem solving. • Planning is everything. • It is important to define the vision and mission clearly: - This is where we want to go. - We want you to be part of it. - We can do this together. - It should be both challenging and fun. • Begin the process of communication and getting players to buy in to shared ownership of achieving the vision. • Coaches do not offer too much input at this stage; it's a time for building informal social relationships.	• Recruit players who have the experience or potential to become involved in a demanding team venture. • Communication, the major problem initially, moves from formal and coach led to informal and player led. • First meeting, first impressions, and the skills of the coach are important in selling the challenge. • An atmosphere of competitive tension will exist at this stage as players informally rank their ability levels. • Players may buy in at this stage, but personal agendas ("What's in it for me?") will still dominate over any team agenda. • Establish house rules to mark boundaries for behavior.

Coaches and players can check their responsibilities in contributing to the process of team coherence by examining tables 10.1, 10.2, 10.3, and 10.4. In these tables, I have followed the team-building structure of forming, storming, norming, and performing, but at each stage I have tried to identify important aspects of both task and social cohesion. Of course, many coaches inherit teams

TABLE 10.2 STORMING—PLAYERS BID FOR PLACES ON THE TEAM

Stage 2 Storming: players find their place, role, and status within the team

TASK COHESION	SOCIAL COHESION
• The staff are role models and they must stay strong in this difficult period. • The team plan is now taking shape with specific objectives and identification of players for different roles and responsibilities. Coaches must ensure that everyone has a role and then persuade the player to buy in to the plan. Coaches must manage emotional reactions and tensions and must maintain a high level of communication through regular, relevant team meetings and one-on-one counseling. Coaches must focus on the controllables and manage the team environment to minimize disturbance and distraction. Coaches review and redefine each player's role as far as possible to create a working win-win situation. Coaches manage or "lose" the rebels. The team begins to build its image —name, dress, and so forth.	• This is an emotional time for players as they discover their allotted role and status within the team. • With the internal competition for places comes the threat of - power struggles in the leadership vacuum, - formation of cliques and rivalries, - anticoach attitudes, and - noncommunication from the disaffected. • A number of players will accept and identify with the roles allocated and will begin to move from a personal agenda to a team agenda, from "me" to "we." • Star players may seek special treatment. • Players will establish informal networks of communication. • Coaches should be careful with shared room allocations. • Players' individual personalities will emerge, and coaches will begin to see who will be high maintenance and who will be low maintenance. • Players need help from coaches or counselors at this stage to become more self-aware and to understand others.

who may be in any of the stages described. The tables can be of great help to them in assessing a team's present level of coherence and what steps they might take to improve it.

TABLE 10.3 THE TEAM NORMS AND SETS ASIDE DIFFERENCES

Stage 3 Norming: players start to take responsibility and perform their roles, and the team takes shape

TASK COHESION	SOCIAL COHESION
• The mission statement or core covenant—"the way we will do things as a team"—is agreed upon.	• Players have good understanding of the coaches' philosophy and tactics and their specific roles.
• Relevant, regular practice defines the way the team wants to play and begins to develop - clarity of tactics and roles, - well-understood routines, - specific job descriptions for individual players, - heavy focus on common goals, - a strong team work ethic, - agreed working procedures, and - improved team balance with better role integration.	• Through the physical proximity of practice a social structure emerges: - a captain is chosen, - team leaders develop, - the pecking order of ability becomes clear, - friendship bonding occurs, and - players now give and receive help. • The superordinate goal of beating the opposition creates unity behind a common purpose.
• Coaches must provide constant reinforcement and high levels of feedback.	• Players are now willing to conform, balancing their individual needs with the needs of other team members.
• Coaches must logically match objectives to potential if there is a discrepancy; weaknesses must not be covered up.	• Players display greater appreciation and respect for the various roles on the team.
• Coaches must be proactive in dealing with the hot spots (team problems) and empower players in agreeing to the solution.	• Confidence improves, and the players learn to change negatives into positives. • Players accept greater accountability for their contribution to the team.
• Coaches should sell, not yell, and maintain high levels of communication and sharing with the players.	• Special care must be given to anyone still isolated at this stage.
• Coaches must develop a professional environment with minimal distractions and disruptions.	• Family and friends are taken care of so they can fully support the player.

TABLE 10.4 THE TEAM PERFORMS WITH COHERENCE

Stage 4 Performing: the team cooperates to achieve competition goals

TASK COHESION	SOCIAL COHESION
• The team is now tightly organized and structured. • Coaches and players are fully committed. • Coaches provide strong leadership. • Coaches keep the vision in front of the players. • Coaches appreciate individual effort but reward the team for any success. • Continuity of selection helps stability. • A cooperative but competitive tension exists. • Coaches now understand how to motivate each player. • Coaches will keep listening to players, especially senior players, so they don't miss mood changes or other developments. • The team will now have a culture that will allow it to survive setbacks, learn from them, let go, and move on. • Coaches must remain proactive and deal with problems early. • Coaches will avoid overtraining and remember the value of fun as a way to influence mood. • New recruits must be checked carefully to protect the team ethos. • Everyone must keep learning.	• The team is now beginning to feel distinctive, and players are committed to its development. • Each player accepts his or her role and responsibility to - put the team first, - sacrifice when necessary, - be prepared to help teammates, - socialize with the team, - conform to team rules, and - accept valid criticism. • Intrinsic motivation is high, and players are glad to be part of this team. • Trust and honesty are high. • Players are coping better with emotional lows—nonselection, injury, and so forth. • The development process has left players mentally tougher to deal with the unexpected dilemmas of the game. • Victory or defeat will not disrupt cohesion. • Players are fully accountable for their actions, and the price of failure is high. • Some players may not have bonded—players from different cultures, new players, injured players. The team and coaches must cooperate to solve this.

The Challenge for the Player

When Michael Jordan first joined the Chicago Bulls basketball team, Coach Phil Jackson recognized his unique talent but also saw the effect it was having on the rest of the team. Michael was so good and wanted the ball so much that the other players suffered a decline in motivation and perceived status. The team began to lose cohesion and games.

The problem was solved by a remark from Coach Jackson's mentor, veteran coach Tex Winter, who described Jordan as "good but not great." Michael demanded to know why, and Coach Winter explained that good players in team games only become great when they make players around them better. Once Michael absorbed this, he adapted his game to involve his teammates more. The players came together behind his leadership, and a championship team was born.

So the challenge for the team player is to give up some aspects of a personal agenda—recognition, comfort, rewards—to meet the needs of the team agenda and the potential return of even greater success. The successful coach will identify and take care of each player's personal agenda in order to persuade him or her to commit to the team philosophy.

We can find many examples in which a player benefits greatly by moving from a preoccupation with "me" to a concern for "we." Robbie Van der Laan, a Dutch player for Derby, was technically limited but became a giant on the pitch because of his leadership, communication skills, and enormous positive impact on the players around him.

The highly respected coach and team builder Rinus Michels (1996) describes team building as a structured process in which the coach sets parameters and encourages player involvement but emphasizes that the quality and maturity of the players finally determines the destiny of the team. This is the reason I believe cohesive teams contain senior players—a core who have matured with experience and whose presence can give the team character and stability. American football coach Chuck Noll (Walsh 1998) confirms this: "On every team there is a core group that sets the tone for everybody else. If the tone is positive, you have half the battle won. If negative, you are beaten before you ever walk on the field."

The player who cannot make the move from "me" to "we" suffers what Pat Riley (1993) aptly calls the "disease of me." When this disease spreads through the team, several conditions can occur:

- Collapse of team commitment
- Team sabotage (loss of emotional balance)
- The team dividing against itself
- The team doing just enough to get by
- Players who create 20 percent of the results believing they deserve 80 percent of the rewards

Players must learn to recognize and avoid these negatives. They must work to achieve an acceptable balance between personal and team needs. Tables 10.1, 10.2, 10.3, and 10.4 identify contributions players can make to avoid the "disease of me."

The Challenge for the Coach

The coach is instrumental to team cohesion because he or she is the central point of all communication and has the power and authority to make changes. To maintain such cohesion under the pressure of a soccer season, the coach must display a consistent approach to players and their contribution to the team. N. McLean (Morris and Summers 1995) reminds us that creating team cohesion is an everyday strategy based on a clear philosophy.

> The bag of tricks approach to team building will be unlikely to establish a strong group ethos. On the contrary, successful teams are generally built around a philosophy that emphasises development of the individual, involvement and empowerment of team members, and accountability of individuals for their actions within the team.

The coach must have leadership qualities and must be an inspirational role model who can win the respect of players, create a future vision that excites the team, and create an environment in which players willingly sacrifice and play for each other. When Jack Rowell became coach of the England rugby team, he explained his style of leadership:

> The ability to motivate is crucial to leadership—you have to show them the promised land, and how to get there. So in the

> early days of establishing your position you have to set objectives that are tough, but achievable in the short term and which quickly give people the feeling they can win.

Personal agendas, of course, are important for players, and it is the clever coach who works hard to give players the rewards, identity, care, and attention they are seeking. Then the way is clear for the coach to persuade the player to commit to team philosophy. This is never more difficult than when dealing with the star player. A combination of strong coaching plus pressure from teammates can be the only factors that prevent a "personality player"—much to be desired—from succumbing to the "disease of me" and destroying the team.

Table 10.5 offers guidelines for coaches to help them with the challenge of building team cohesion.

TABLE 10.5 GUIDELINES FOR BUILDING TEAM COHESION

- Establish a team credo—a description that is binding.
- Sell the dream and share ownership with the players.
- Establish honesty and trust between players and coaches.
- Show composure on all issues and maintain emotional balance.
- Make playing for your team special—create image and identity.
- Maximize the value of anything positive that happens.
- Minimize the impact of anything negative.
- Increase communication and decrease anxiety.
- Build a player core by continuity of selection and loyalty.
- Challenge all players to be the best they can be.
- Seek leadership from within the team.
- Build togetherness through the hard work of preparation.
- Be proactive in dealing with problems.
- Use bonding exercises to create team chemistry.
- Learn from every experience—embrace victory or defeat.
- Constantly feed the players images of success.
- Balance work, rest, and recovery.
- Demonstrate this positive approach with all staff involved with the team.
- Control the environment, allowing in only what helps.

Summary

A group becomes a team when the players unite to achieve a purpose and work together cohesively. Such development, never easy in the challenging environment of soccer, depends highly on the mental and emotional stability of players and coaches.

Players and coaches are challenged to be part of both task cohesion, knowing and doing their jobs well, and social cohesion, being able to integrate and contribute to team relationships. The four stages of team building—forming, storming, norming, and performing—are reviewed as are the actions that coaches and players should take to build a unified and cohesive team.

A Japanese proverb can summarize this chapter: "None of us are as smart as all of us."

chapter

11

Coaching

Changing the Culture

What I try to do, is create an environment in which it's possible to succeed. Football is a constant education. I present ideas, not mandates, and try to take advantage of the good people we have. A good coach has to constantly adjust.

George Seifert, American football coach

Coaching the reserve team is always a difficult job, so it was with interest that I observed the changes in the reserve team at Derby County when Steve Round—a young, forward-looking coach—was appointed to lead them.

Within a month he had changed the culture of the team completely by sharing with the players a series of steps designed to change their perceptions of playing on the reserves:

- They agreed on their mission statement as a team: "To focus on player development in order to support and challenge the first team."
- They set team goals for the season, such as
  - earning the trust and respect of senior players and staff,
  - being a developmental and learning team, and
  - being a mentally tough team by developing spirit and challenging each other to be better.
- They reviewed the obstacles to success, including
  - poor attitude and lack of communication,
  - lack of belief in self and team, and
  - failure to handle the bad times.

The team now had shared ownership of its destiny. With the vastly increased communication and obvious commitment of Coach Round, suddenly this was an enjoyable team to be on. Team chemistry became strong. Being on the reserves—they now call themselves the second team—was not as good as being on the first team, but it could still be a positive soccer experience.

What Coach Round had done was take coaching beyond a physical and technical exercise—the Xs and Os of soccer—and begin to coach the players as people. By examining their mental and emotional needs and finding a range of coaching strategies to meet them, he changed the culture of a negative reserve-team experience to something positive—a learning environment that reinforced the players' self-identity and self-esteem.

This book has emphasized that successful performance in this changing modern game will increasingly demand better mental, emotional, and lifestyle skills from players. It will also demand coaches who are capable of coaching the mind as well as the body—coaches who are able to understand and access the power of positive mental attitudes.

That's not to say that present coaching is entirely negative or that the future will be entirely positive, but it is true that tradition and culture, especially in Britain, have created a coaching philosophy based on domination, power, and fear. Coaches must be strong, of course, and the time may come when it is acceptable to be angry. But as Aristotle so wisely pointed out:

> Anyone can become angry–
> That is easy.
> But to be angry with the right person,
> To the right degree,
> At the right time,
> For the right purpose,
> And in the right way,
> –This is not easy.

Coaches will have to develop the range of skills that

- meet the needs of a fast-changing, sophisticated game,
- meet the needs of a modern player who demands more selling and may not accept yelling,
- assess and shape the player's mental and emotional state,
- are positive rather than negative, and
- prioritize constant communication both to the team and to individual players.

The Modern Coach

The coach, of course, will always be at the center of change. Already a significant move is occurring from the traditional *technocratic* coach who, according to Gyr (1998), "has a mechanistic view of the game and sees players as part of a machine. They simply direct players in an orderly, systemised way" to the modern *holistic* coach who

> will do the above but also work on the psyche of the players and send out a team whose play involves commitment, intelligence, and control. Holes in the team's mental defences will be treated as of equal importance to weaknesses in the back four.

Table 11.1 shows how coaches can change the culture of their teams without compromising their desire to win games. What is needed is a way of coaching that embraces the modern player in the modern game and creates a shared energy and motivation for greater success. To achieve that, table 11.1 paints a picture of the modern coach as a smart, democratic, player-centered teacher who plans carefully and focuses on the excellence of performance as the way forward. Another point is that the coach should be mentored, not isolated. Just as coaches Steve McLaren and Steve Round shared their ideas with me, others will be willing, even eager, to help young coaches. All coaches need an appropriate mentor.

TABLE 11.1 THE MOVE FROM TRADITIONAL TO MODERN COACHING

Traditional	Modern
Focused on winning	Focused on winning (no change)
Task-centered	Player-centered
Results dominated	Excellence dominated
Instinctive	Careful planning
Player dependent	Coach influenced
Isolated	Mentored
"Me"	"We"
Authoritarian	Democratic
Yells	Sells
Speaks	Listens and then speaks
Trainer	Teacher
Ex-player	Qualified coach
Hard worker	Smart worker

If you already consider yourself a modern holistic coach, then you can check your coaching and leadership style against figure 11.1. Coaches A and B represent the shift from technocratic to holistic, but I always point out that your style should be appropriate to

- the gender, age, ability, and experience of your players,
- the league you are playing in,
- the level of ambition agreed to between coach and players, and
- your personality and what you feel comfortable with.

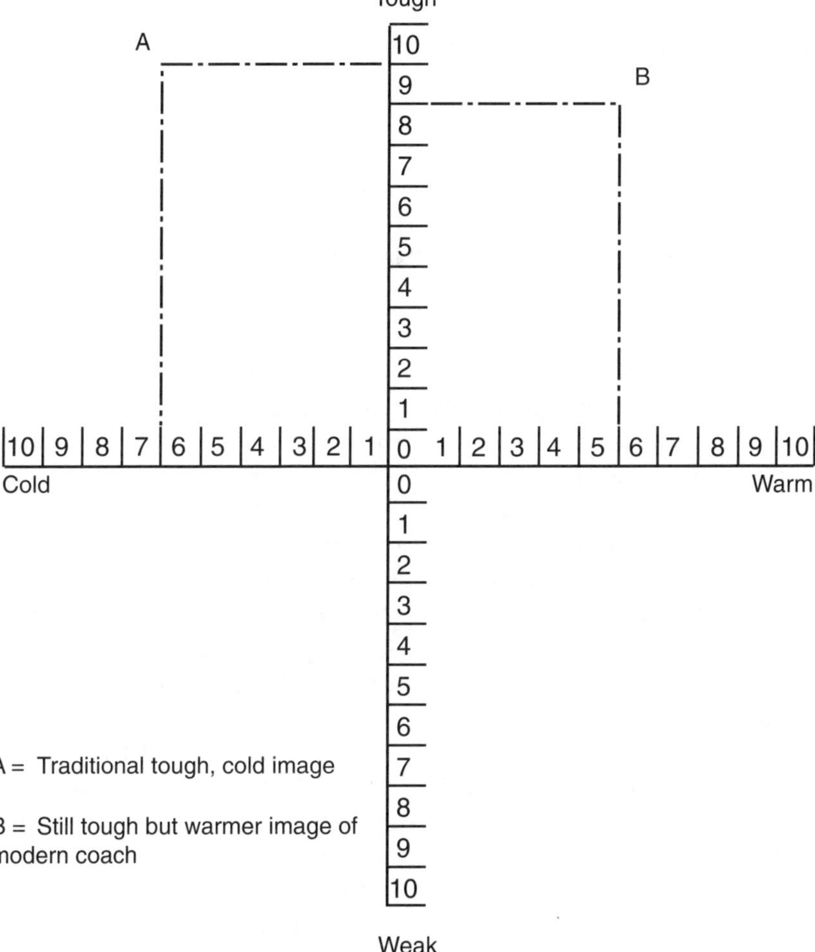

Figure 11.1 To determine your coaching style, rate yourself on the two continuums (1 is very low and 10 is very high) and mark where the scores intersect.

In that sense I would expect coaches of younger players to be far warmer and less tough, a situation in which many young female coaches can excel. Figure 11.1 allows coaches a simplistic, but nonetheless interesting, opportunity to identify the nature of their coaching style. For greater validity, coaches should obtain three independent assessments.

Keys to Modern Coaching

Many coaches, of course, already observe modern philosophy and practice, showing positive enthusiasm, possessing high self-belief, demonstrating fairness and belief in their players, and always recognizing individual effort. These new leaders liberate their players, creating an environment in which players can take responsibility for their performance knowing they will receive care and support if the going gets tough.

To achieve this goal, the modern coach must pursue the process of envisioning, enabling, and empowering.

Envisioning

Players will not accept responsibility for a vision they cannot accept or become enthused about. It is the coach's primary task to set before the team a vision of future achievement through hard work, a team goal that could be met if all players buy into it, and a suitable reward for meeting the challenge. Two former basketball greats emphasize this role of the coach. Bill Bradley (1998) stated that "leadership means getting people to think, believe, see, and do what they might not have without you." Phil Jackson (Jackson and Delehanty 1995) wrote that "the key leadership function of a coach is to get the players to commit to something bigger than themselves."

Modern coaches must take great care in goal setting to ensuring the proper mix of challenge and attainability. The most exciting challenge for Derby County in the English Premier League would be the goal of becoming champions. This vision, however, is so difficult that it might defeat rather than enthuse, so the Derby players and coaches—in a shared process at the preseason training camp—have set four main goals, which unfold as the season progresses:

1. Stay in the league (the bottom three teams are relegated).
2. Have a good Cup run.
3. If progress allows, secure a top-six place and qualification for a European competition.
4. If progress allows, go for the championship.

In the past three seasons Derby has always achieved the first goal, twice attained the second, never quite made it to the third, and has not been close to the fourth. Players and coaches have had no difficulty buying into these goals, which are monitored and re-presented to them regularly during the season. The rewards have been both satisfaction at staying in the league and the excitement and involvement of reaching for the greater challenges. As the team improves its talent base, it gains greater energy to maintain the pursuit of all its goals.

The modern coach will also excite individual players by challenging them to become the best they can be. As a teacher, the coach must ensure the best learning opportunities, feedback, monitoring, and reinforcement.

Whether it be in the media, in team meetings, or in one-on-one sessions, the modern coach is a communicator and an inspirer—a story teller who can enthuse young players with vision and challenge and persuade players to travel together on the difficult road to success.

Enabling

Coaching is taking players somewhere new. If the coach offers the players a vision, he or she must ensure that they have the ability to make the journey. The enabling program will be based on regular observation of each player's strengths and weaknesses, followed by meetings to agree on an action plan for improvement. Players will respond well to the individual attention of the coach. Evidence indicates that some coaches talk to star players seven times more often than they do weaker players, so it is likely that regular and more widespread communication alone will produce immediate improvement in motivation.

Players will be asked to take control of their action plan. Coaches will help players self-reference by beginning discussions with the question, "How do *you* think you are doing?" In this way coaches establish a learning environment in which mistakes and failures are part of the journey to the vision:

> The best coaches are developers of people as lifelong learners. They help the kids embrace the act of becoming better at whatever *they* choose to do or be. And a big part of this is being able to surrender control of the process to the player rather than trying to direct everything from the coach's perch. (Thompson 1995)

Characteristics of the learning environment that we established at Derby County include the following:

- A clear sense of purpose—everything is designed to help achieve the vision.
- Hard work through repetition but, we hope, without boredom.
- The importance of practice—"the destiny of the game is shaped at practice."
- All embracing—we train players to cope mentally, emotionally, and in lifestyle terms as well as physically and technically.
- Feedback is everything. Players are not left isolated. An important part of the coach's job is to provide helpful, honest, and constructive critique.
- Players are constantly bombarded with "best practice" and positive images (often video) they can aspire to.
- When players need expertise beyond what the staff can offer, we provide it without question.

Empowering

The modern player must be persuaded rather than dominated. He or she will react positively to being empowered, to having greater control over personal destiny. Many coaches find this a difficult step to take because their role models are likely to be the authoritarian coaches of tradition and culture. A coach must be secure personally, with high self-belief and strong identity, to loosen some of the reins of power.

The dilemma is that on the one hand a coach may abuse power and on the other the power of the players may be excessive. The solution must be in between. At Derby we have tried to create a coach-led organization that is player centered, one in which discipline is expected on and off the field but where shared ownership encourages the players to be self-disciplined. Table 11.2 allows coaches to check how well they and their teams are doing in creating an environment of shared ownership.

TABLE 11.2 NEW COACHING AND LEADERSHIP

Sample questions to evaluate how your team is working together (rank 1–5, disagree strongly to agree strongly). The higher the sum of your answers the better.

	Disagree	–			Agree
The team knows exactly what its short and long term goals are	1	2	3	4	5
Team members freely express real views and are listened to	1	2	3	4	5
Every team member has a clear idea of their role on the team	1	2	3	4	5
Everyone gets the opportunity to contribute their best	1	2	3	4	5
Team members respect and encourage each other	1	2	3	4	5
All relationships on and supporting the team are constructive	1	2	3	4	5
Where possible decisions are usually by consensus rather than imposed	1	2	3	4	5
Team members are always kept informed of what's going on	1	2	3	4	5
There is little unproductive bickering on the team	1	2	3	4	5
All achievements are recognized and celebrated	1	2	3	4	5
TOTAL (max. 50)					

Lions' Laws

The British Lions rugby tour of South Africa in 1997 produced a seminar on modern holistic coaching by Ian McGeechan and Jim Telfer—the video is a must for coaches. Players were provided a vision, enabled, and empowered every step of the way. They reacted to this process of shared ownership so powerfully that the team achieved every objective for the tour and defeated the world champions in their own country.

The players and coaches took part in a team-bonding preparation week in which they had to work together to overcome the challenges of the great outdoors. This produced a list of words that helped individuals and the team be successful. These became the Lions' Laws—watchwords that would guide the commitment, attitude, and behavior of everyone on the tour.

Winners leads the list, but the other words demonstrate what modern players feel they can commit to.

Lions' Laws—Watchwords of the Tour:

- Winners
- Honesty
- Highest standards
- Enjoyment
- Discipline (self and team)
- Positive
- Desire
- Constructive
- Identity
- United
- Dedication
- Committed
- Cohesiveness
- Flexible
- Supportive
- Respect (personal space)
- Trust
- Punctual
- Openness
- No cliques

In the end the strongest motivation must be because the player wants to win. In a team sport, the motivation must be because the players want to win together. The best way of encouraging this is to allow players as much power as possible in creating the learning and winning environment.

If a coach cannot persuade players to buy into a team agenda or if a coach resorts to bullying, players will withdraw even more deeply into their personal agendas. Chapter 10 describes Pat Riley's (1993) warning of the "disease of me" in graphic detail, and Phil Jackson (in Bradley 1998) illustrates this with the story of the player who broke ranks with the team because of a selfish attitude. When the team settled back into the locker room after the game, Coach Jackson said to the team, "I think you have something to say to this guy," and then left the room. He was empowering his team to enforce self-discipline through peer pressure.

Summary

This book encourages players and coaches to include mental and emotional skills in their search for excellence, in their quest to become complete players and be part of a successful team. With the changing demands of the modern game and the modern player, this dictates a shift from traditional technocratic coaching to a holistic style in which players are offered a vision, enabled, and empowered to share ownership with the coach on their journey to excellence.

Coaches must develop the philosophy and skill to change the culture of their teams, to gain access to the power of positive attitudes, and to influence change from negative to positive, hope to belief, and fear to confidence.

references

Botterill, C., and Patrick, T. 1996. *Human Potential.* Winnipeg: Lifeskills.

Bradley, B. 1998. *Values of the Game.* New York: Artisan.

Carron, A.V. 1988. *Group Dynamics in Sports: Theoretical and Practical Issues.* London, Ontario: Spodyn.

Courtenay, B. 1989. *The Power of One.* London: Heineman-Mandarin.

Covey, S.R. 1989. *The 7 Habits of Highly Effective People.* New York: Simon and Schuster.

Gilbourne, D. 1999. *Insight—The Football Association Coaches Journal* 2: 37.

Goldberg, A.S. 1998. *Sports Slump Busting.* Champaign, IL: Human Kinetics.

Goleman, D. 1995. *Emotional Intelligence.* London: Bloomsbury.

Green, E., and Green, A. 1977. *Beyond Biofeedback.* New York: Dial Press.

Gyr, P. 1998. "Getting Players to Take Psychological Responsibility." *FIFA Magazine* (February).

Halberstam, D. 1999. *Playing for Keeps.* New York: Random House.

Holtz, L., with Heisler, J. 1989. *A Championship Season at Notre Dame.* New York: Pocket Books.

Isberg, L. 1997. *Insight—The Football Association Coaches Journal* 1: 16.

Jackson, P., and Delehanty, H. 1995. *Sacred Hoops.* New York: Hyperion.

Jenner, B. 1996. *Finding the Champion Within.* New York: Simon and Schuster.

Johnson, M. 1996. *Slaying the Dragon.* U.K.: Judy Piatkur.

Jordan, M. 1994. *I Can't Accept Not Trying.* New York: Harper Collins.

Kramer, J., ed. 1970. *Lombardi: Winning Is the Only Thing.* New York: World.

Loehr, J.E., and McLaughlin, P.J. 1990. *Mental Toughness Training.* Chicago: Nightingale Conant.

Lombardi, V. 1996. *Coaching for Teamwork.* Bellevue, WA: Reinforcement.

Lynch, G.P. 1986. *Super Performances for Runners and Other Athletes.* Englewood Cliffs, NJ: Prentice-Hall.

Michels, R. 1996. "Team-Building." Presented at the 2nd European Coaches Convention. U.E.F.A. Lecture Series No. 2.

Miller, B. 1997. *Gold Minds—The Psychology of Winning in Sport.* England: Crowood Press Ltd.

Morris, T., and Summers, J., eds. 1995. *Sport Psychology: Theory, Applications, and Issues.* Queensland: John Wiley.

Nelson, M.B. 1998. *Embracing Victory: Life's Lessons in Competition and Compassion.* New York: Morrow.

Orlick, T. 1986. *Psyching for Sport.* Champaign, IL: Human Kinetics.

Parcells, B. 1995. *Finding a Way to Win.* New York: Doubleday.

Pitino, R. 1997. *Success Is a Choice.* New York: Broadway.

Ravizza, K., and Hanson, T. 1995. *Heads Up Baseball.* Indianapolis: Masters Press.

Reardon, J. 1998. "Sports Psychology and Soccer." Conference presentation, Warrington.

Riley, P. 1993. *The Winner Within.* New York: Berkley.

Shula, D., and Blanchard, K. 1995. *Everyone's a Coach.* Grand Rapids, MI: Zondervan.

Taylor, J. 1998. "Focus and Intensity for Training and Competition." Presentation at 1998 conference of the Association for the Advancement of Applied Sports Psychology.

Thompson, J. 1995. *Positive Coaching.* Portola Valley, CA: Warde.

Tuckman, B.W. 1965. "Development Sequence in Small Groups." *Psychological Bulletin* 63: 384–399.

Walsh, B. 1998. *Finding the Winning Edge.* Champaign, IL: Sports Publishing.

Wooden, J. 1972. *They Call Me Coach: As Told to Jack Tobin.* Waco, TX: Word Books.

index

Note: The italicized *f* and *t* following page numbers refer to figures and tables, respectively.

about the author

Bill Beswick is a leader in the field of applied sport psychology. With a master's of education and a background as the head coach of England's men's basketball team, Bill became the first sport psychology consultant to operate full time in English professional soccer.

For the last four seasons, Beswick has helped the Derby County Football Club compete successfully in one of the world's toughest soccer leagues—the English Premier League. The English Football Association recognized Beswick's accomplishments there and appointed him as their first-ever sport psychology consultant to advise their national teams.

Beswick is the owner and managing director of SportsMind, a company dedicated to the further development of applied sport psychology in all sports. He is also an active member of the Association for the Advancement of Applied Sports Psychology. Bill currently resides in Cheshire, England, and enjoys keeping fit, reading, traveling, and watching his son play rugby.